THE TRUTH OF LOVE

THE TRUE STORY OF ONE WOMAN'S SPIRITUAL AWAKENING AMIDST A COUNTRY AT WAR

BY TY CHAMBERS

For you dear reader and all my other brothers and sisters:

God,

Help us to remember that we are all equal in your eyes.

Amen

Table of Contents

Chapter 1

"And for this I hate Jesus of Nazareth who caused me to be alone in this
unploughed field and this withered garden."

***Jesus The Son Of Man*, Kahlil Gibran**

July 1999

I heard the sound of water rushing through pipes and realized I didn't have much time. He was in the shower. If I was going to do this, it had to be quick. I rooted around in my bag and found the bottle. No, the water hadn't leaked. That was good. I couldn't afford to waste a drop of it. I had left it outside under a full moon in a bowl filled with seashells and I had said words over it - special words, filled with intention and longing. I opened the door to the back garden and tipped some of the magical liquid onto his doorstep. Then I ran to the front door, swung it open and poured the rest of the water there. As I turned to close it, he was before me, towel wrapped around his body and dripping hair. Oliver. My boyfriend.

"Forgot my comb…" he stopped, glancing at my hurried attempt to close the door.

"Thought I heard a knock," I said nonchalantly, empty bottle behind my back. He shrugged and headed back upstairs. Pleased with myself I sat down, shoved it into my bag and reckoned *if that didn't make him miss me on his trip to Spain with his playboy cousin, nothing would.*

A few days later, after Oliver had left for his cousin's villa in the mountains I got a phone call at three in the morning. It took me a while to realize it was him. The phone had woken me from a dead sleep.

"Tina! Are you there? Tina?" Strange. I could hear dogs barking in the background: a lot of dogs.

"Err yeah, it's me. Are you okay? It's three in the bloody morning. What's happened?" I mumbled, barely awake but still, a little frightened. *Had something bad happened to him?*

"I …miss you so much… I just miss you. I love you Tina." I closed my eyes and threw myself back onto my pillows, exhaling loudly into the phone so that Oliver would hear my frustration.

"Huh? You woke me just to tell me that? And why on earth are there so many dogs in the background? What's going on?"

"Umm… wild dogs. They've just chased me across the mountains. But I don't care. I would do anything to speak to you my darling. My love. I love you." My eyes widened in fear and I almost yelled,

"Wild dogs are chasing you? What the fuck Oliver!"

"I ran for an hour to the nearest phone box." He continued. "I don't really know why, but I just had to call you. My cousin says I'm no fun and all I do is talk about how much I miss you."

Oh Goddess I thought. *The spell!* Every night for the rest of his time in Spain, he insisted on calling me several times a day - most of the time after midnight. He came across needy and annoying. I was seventeen. He was seventeen. Our immature relationship didn't last much longer. Let's just call it a lesson learnt. He was my first boyfriend. I was stupid. Witches make mistakes too. Yes I said *witch.* There are many all around the world, part of this ancient nature-based tradition that has only grown in numbers over the past twenty years.

For a witch, herbs aren't just for eating and brooms aren't just for cleaning. They can be tools for creating our own life paths. Within witchcraft, life isn't like surfing a wave and going where it takes you. There is no life experience that has not been carved out by us. We hold the keys to our destinies. We are co-creators of the universe with the divine. Witches do not worship plants or animals but recognize a fragment of the divine within them just as they recognize it in each other as brothers and sisters. If you enter witchcraft for the right reasons, it can be freeing if not enlightening. It has been part of my soul since the age of twelve.

My parents were somewhat perplexed by my embracing of a spiritual path at such a tender age, especially considering the fact that they were both atheist at that time. Stranger still, my father is Turkish and from a secular Muslim background and my mother, of English, Catholic heritage. In order for both of them to fulfill social expectations I remember fasting during Ramadan when I was a child and excitedly putting up a tree at Christmas. Despite the well - intentioned attempts to give my two younger sisters and I the material things our friends had (money at Eid and presents at Christmas), which of course I loved, I was aware that there was something missing. I realized later that it was *God*. Like *Lord Voldemort* in the '*Harry Potter*' stories, it was a 'He who shall not be named' sort of figure in our house. A dirty word almost. I don't recall ever hearing talk of anything spiritual in my childhood and so I rarely thought of Him but I did wonder why we celebrated Christmas without church and Eid without a mosque.

The truth was that my parents had me when they were both nineteen years old. My mum a child of the seventies and my dad a product of the Turkish revolution, they were both from an era when young people fought to be heard and in my dad's case, fought to survive. I grew up hearing tales of the 1980 Turkish Military Coup and how my father had to flee Istanbul to Devon, England to continue his study of mathematics. Under army rule, university students were eyed with suspicion and many were taken to jail for reading a certain book or just went missing altogether. The military leaders aimed to discourage these young people from questioning, criticizing and analyzing the actions of this new renegade government. So there was no time for my father to consider God. There was only the will to survive and to be free.

In Exeter my parents first met, had me, married, had two more children and entered a new cycle of struggling to financially support their own family whilst my dad was still studying to be a teacher and my mum raised me, and two sisters at home. There was no time to contemplate the meaning of life. For my mother, she had grown up with an uncaring, absent father. Often interpreting her life as harsh and unfair, she had concluded that God did not exist. It was the eighties. There was music and dancing and outrageous fashions. There was no place for God. God *was* harsh and unfair. God put people in prison for fighting for their rights. God created unloving fathers and made little, innocent girls suffer at their hands. This is the God I learnt of and like judging someone before you've even met him, I was convinced He was no good and so I was inspired to look elsewhere for the answers to my questions; the usual, childish questions that only a youngster has the time to worry about. Like where had the Earth come from, who created us, and what happened to people when they died. I found them in witchcraft and paganism.

My introduction to witchcraft had humble beginnings. As a twelve year old I had an obsession with the woods. My parents would drive us all up to Epping Forest (we had moved to London by then) and I remember picking up leaves and stones and holding them in my hands, willing them to speak to me. I kept a tiny table in the corner of my room that I decorated with seasonal flowers and fruits, which I now know was my version of an altar. Not only did I develop my own conversation with nature itself but also I was aware of an immense calling to the unknown. I would look out of my window, up into dark skies for hours, just listening. And there was something important hidden amongst the depths of a wood. Black and secretive it resided there. If only I could discover what it was.

It wasn't until I was in my late teens that I stumbled upon the concept of the Goddess. I had just learnt of the Mind, Body, Soul section, in my local bookshop. It consisted of one dusty bookshelf located way at the back of the store. I would huddle there, cross-legged on the floor, devouring book after book on this mysterious woman. I learnt how she is the Earth – giver of life, and holds the same power to take life away. I discovered that she lives in the moon, and represents a woman in all her life cycle. New moon the maiden, full moon the mother and waning moon the crone. The

Goddess is all the beauty and light on a spring day but yet equally the leafless tree on a winter's night. She is the gentle mother but has the potential to be a fierce protector. I learnt from books and poetry that this woman has depths unknown. I immediately loved Her and everything She stood for.

Looking back I believe I readily chose to identify with the Goddess, rather than God, as a masculine, religious figure because the Goddess seemed more tangible somehow. I could walk barefoot on grass and feel Her steady me. When I was thirsty, I was able to sense Her water flowing into my body and sustaining me. I was capable of breathing Her in and touching Her with my fingers. Her ability to create and bring forth life was mirrored in me. Her three faces – maiden, mother and crone – were my future. So who was God? I didn't know. I had no room for Him and His stuffy attitude toward women anyway. In paganism the woman is a goddess. My monthly cycle is a blessing that allows me to create life in the same way the Divine does but in Islam, a menstruating woman is deemed 'unclean'. In paganism, being a woman is a gift but according to the Bible, women are the carriers of original sin. I wondered whom this man was in the sky that had proclaimed me second to men. It was as though my chance in life had been taken away before it had even started. According to the patriarchal God present in religion, I was born 'bad' and naturally, I only grew to dislike Him more and more.

Despite my love and dedication to the Goddess however, I struggled to reconcile my practice with, 'growing up.' All my friends had started drinking alcohol and having nights out at the pub. If I wanted to keep them in my life I had to start neglecting my daily walks in the woods and evening meditations didn't I? When I became a student at Kent University I put witchcraft on the backburner. I slowly edged out of the forest and into the local nightclub, partying with friends and kissing boys – a great distraction from all that spiritual stuff and as a result I was quite lost in the couple of years after graduation. I moved back in with my parents in London and tried to figure out what I was supposed to be doing with my life. Despite coming away from Kent with a degree in clinical psychology, I went into teaching. I got a job as a lecturer in an East London college and wiled away my days helping refugees and asylum seekers to learn English. It was a satisfying, rewarding job but on a particularly beautiful spring day, when pink and white marshmallows blossomed in tree branches and apples would land with a thud on the ground in September sunshine, I would reflect on the Goddess again and wonder if She had forgotten me.

Then, in 2005, at the age of twenty-three I met Ryan. I had started having panic attacks by then. Full-blown, dizzying spells of breathlessness and anxiety. I was confined to the house most of the time and joined what would now be termed a social media site but this was before *facebook.* People uploaded pictures and wrote about themselves and when I came across his profile I was stunned by the beauty in his eyes. I discerned immediately that he too was searching for something. I on the other hand had not been able to figure out how to upload photos to my account and so we chatted for three weeks, he not knowing what I looked like. “Twinkle, twinkle little star…” he wrote. I didn't want to leave him wondering anymore. Both living in London, we met up. I kept the red rose he greeted me with for years afterwards. He cooked me a meal and we fell immediately into a relationship that was more than I could ever wish for and for some reason my panic attacks subsided.

Ryan was one day, one month and one year older than I was and lived with his mum and her two children from a different father. He worked in a bar when we first met but he was convinced that life had more to offer him. He was a creative: a photographer, a director, an actor and a writer and his faith in life, in turn lit up mine. Between us we didn't have much money but we had great parents who allowed us to live at home. For me personally, it wasn't about money, it was about being together. There was something about this man: as though he was being carried through life in the arms of the Divine. Ryan had survived so much adversity from such a young age, not only at home and illness (he had severe asthma) but on the streets as well. Being a black male living in a predominately white area of London during the eighties brought him his fair share of trouble too. At the age of eight a man affiliated with the British National Party (a far right, unregistered political party) stabbed him in a racist attack. He told me of running to his front door with blood gushing out of a hole in his little, bony leg. It was due to these instances that I was aware he was going to be somebody important one day. I figured that the average young male might be angry about the unjustness of it all and make angry life choices. Not Ryan. His goal in life was to be able to take care of his mother someday and when he wasn't pondering the meaning of the universe, considering some new creative endeavor and giving me his pensive look, his face was ninety-five percent, teeth! He was always ready to burst into laughter; truly an inspirational guy, admiring him as well as loving him made all of our intimate moments together that much more special.

Chapter 2

It turned out that I was right about his search for something. In stark contrast to my own upbringing, Ryan had been raised in a strict Christian family. His mother had him standing outside Westminster Abbey every day after school handing out pamphlets to passers-by.

“Jesus died for you!” he would shout in his small five-year-old voice and people would look at him, shake their heads at his mother and keep walking. When I allowed Ryan into my life he brought with him, his fear of Satan and ending up in Hell. A concept that seemed ridiculous to me. In witchcraft we have no hateful father who watches our every move, just so that he can catch us out and throw us into an infernal, fiery pit for making a few mistakes. The path of the Goddess teaches that just as we have light within us, so do we have dark. It is our responsibility to do what is right for ourselves and for those around us. Many witches have adopted the Eastern philosophies of karma and accept that if you harm someone, the harm you have caused will come back to you threefold. Myself and others who are guided by the ways of our ancient ancestors, do not envisage Eastern ideas as having a bearing on the British version of this old way of living. I don't need doctrine and rules to tell me that to purposely hurt someone is wrong.

I always figured that either the Divine should have more faith in us or that we should have more faith in each other.

My relationship with Ryan was also peppered with bouts of fear regarding sex and sexuality, drilled into him by the church. Although everything was always great in that department between us, the topic occasionally arose. Having sex out of wedlock was wrong. Sex was for one purpose and one purpose only: making babies. Get the filthy deed over and done with. Have a shower. *Now I am worthy of God again.* So I thought I had better not tell him about Beltane. The ancient fertility rites that were performed by our ancestors on the first of May as a celebration of that holy, intrinsic joining of two people, called sex. A fire festival, there are marriages performed outside and people lie in the grass warmed by bonfires, making love to represent the joining of the God and Goddess and celebrating the life that fosters their union. This life that can be seen in the trees and flowers and cattle. How strange it was to me, that Ryan saw wrongdoing where I saw sacred and fear where I saw mystery.

In the first few months of our relationship, Ryan started to talk about searching for a path to God (whoever that was), and told me that he had converted to Islam before in the search to find Him but had not been successful. So he branched out from mainstream religion and began immersing himself in meditation, *new thought* and the teachings of several influential authors such as *Wayne Dyer* and *Michael Beckwith,* which put him on the road to self-discovery. The realization that I missed the Goddess after my few years at university also played on my mind so I started connecting to nature again.

The spiritual journey Ryan and I embarked upon brought us closer together. Every evening we would share any new lessons we had gleaned throughout the day in excitement. I knew I had finally found a kindred spirit, someone with the same passionate longing to fill that void where we should be feeling divine energy but don't because we are all too distracted by life. For he and I, we had a physical ache for it. We had both had unexplained, spiritual experiences since childhood and we both knew that our lives would never truly be peaceful until we had found a way to grasp that higher energy. So together, albeit in different ways, we resumed *the search.*

By the time I was twenty-five, I was a Goddess loving, barefoot dancing, green tea drinking hippy and I lived in my own little world. I held my own workshops in North West London where I taught herbal magic, tarot and spiritual chakra dance for women and at twenty-six, Ryan was working full time for a family media company and had started his own spiritual life coaching business. He taught visualization techniques and encouraged clients to utilize moments of stillness to improve their lives, whilst I advised my ladies to dance for what they wanted!

Although his take on spirituality seemed the very antithesis of mine, I liked it like that. I loved him for his masculinity. We complimented each other. Everyday was like Beltane – we were a physical expression of the coming together of the God and the Goddess and because of it our relationship seemed holier than before. We had spoken of marriage and children and living together and now that we both had a steady income what was once a dream for us was turning into a reality.

Chapter 3

I found what I was looking for on a small bookshelf that was lined with dozens of copies of 'A Course in Miracles'. Amidst the sea of indigo and gold was the hardback version including workbook for students and manual for teachers. *That's what Ryan said he wanted,* I thought as I confidently reached for it. *Ouch! Thirty quid? A bit pricey for a book that sort of looks like any other.* I remember clearly what I did next. I hugged the book to my chest and walked towards the cashier to pay. I am not sure why I would have such an intimate moment with a book that meant nothing to me. In fact, I had no clue what it was about. Why would I? It wasn't about magic or spells. There was nothing fantastical about it. I dismissed it as soon as I saw the cover as one of Ryan's logical 'man texts'. So what happened next surprised me and I can still recall every second of the moment to this day, some eight years later. A conscious awareness of calm, peace and happiness descended on me and I acknowledged it, knowing that there was something 'strange' about this book. The book struck me as being a messenger of a million thoughts, with the objective to communicate them straight to my heart. Looking back now, I am convinced that it spoke to me that evening but as I got home, wrapped it and put it in a bag to give to Ryan, I had no clue that it would indeed express to me all it had to say. *A Course in Miracles* was about to send me on a spiritual journey that would be so different to all that I had ever known or experienced and it wasn't even *my* book.

Chapter 4

“I can’t do this book Tina.” I was on the phone with Ryan, amused.

“You’ve thrown it against the wall haven’t you?” I asked, a smile forming at the corners of my mouth. That's what he always did either when he found a book exciting or when he was frustrated with it. There was silence and then a slow,

“Yeah.” I can’t say I wasn't glad to hear this news.

Ryan had been acting weird ever since he had started doing the daily lessons (one for every day of the year) in *A Course in Miracles*. He was mumbling about special relationships and how nothing really had any meaning. By this time I had gathered that the mysterious book had some sort of way of living in there that he and I had never encountered before. Nothing he said seemed to make sense to me when he tried to explain. Once he told me it said that people should only seek a relationship with God and that all earthly relationships are meaningless. I didn't like the sound of that. I advised him to stop reading the book but he continued doing these so called ‘lessons’ and now he was on the phone, his ego somewhat defeated. He had failed at completing a spiritual journey. Or so he and I had thought at the time. I decided I needed to understand a bit about this book if I were going to fight it. *Keep your friends close but your enemies closer,* I remembered. I asked:

"What's it about anyway? I know you've said some stuff about it but who wrote it and what's their point? You were so happy when I gave it to you. Now you're miserable."

"It's really awesome Tina I promise you. I just know if I gave it a bit more time, I might actually be…" his voice trailed off.

"What?" I said, growing impatient.

"Enlightened." Ryan had become enthralled recently with the notion that he could study to be enlightened. That's what I fancied he was essentially doing. Reading books in the hopes that another human being might allow him to gain enlightenment through their experiences rather than actually encourage him to reach for his own. I took a deep breath, actively tried to not roll my eyes, did it anyway and pressed for more answers.

"What do you mean? Tell me." I sat down in my computer chair, ready for the story and picked up my favorite crystal as I tried to get comfortable. A Lapis Lazuli. A friend had bought it for me in New York. I loved these indigo colored stones… *reminds me of something ancient and powerful. They remind me of a life I used to be part of...* Ryan's voice brings me back to the here and now.

"… This man and woman back in the sixties … or was it the seventies? Hmmm… anyway they decided to work together to figure out another way to deal with the negative atmosphere that had formed between colleagues in their workplace. They both worked in the same university in the States. The man seemed to be more spiritual than her. She didn't believe in God at all. In fact, she hated God because she had spent many years of her early adulthood searching for Him but she felt He didn't put in as much effort as she did!" Ryan laughed and commented that he could definitely relate to that whilst I snuck a smug peek at the altar that I had dedicated to the winter season in the corner of my bedroom. It was covered with branches of red berries and sprigs of holly on a white cloth. A small dish of water held white icy crystals and a white candle stood, waiting to be lit. It was so comforting to me that I could find the Divine everywhere if I tried, although I understood I hadn't fully discovered the Goddess within me yet and that was a huge part of being a spiritual witch. *That would come eventually*, I thought. *Right?*

"So anyway," he continued. "She started having dreams and visions and recorded them until one day she called the guy, claiming that she could hear a voice talking to her and that he had said his name was Jesus. The teachings he relayed to her are here, in the book."

I gasped.

“So it’s like the Bible then?”

“Not at all actually. The Jesus from *A Course in Miracles* explains points in the Bible that he feels has been misinterpreted in some way. And he also says that it isn’t necessary for the reader to accept that the words in the book belong to the figure we know as Jesus.”

“Aww, poor Jesus.” I sighed. “He knows people these days have issues with him!” Ryan laughed again.

“Yeah. True story!” He paused. “Tina. This book is making me think. I am not sure if being in a relationship is right… don't get upset. I just mean I am not sure if I will ever be able to reach enlightenment in a relationship… Jesus says that we…”

“Ryan!” I interjected with a squeal of horror. “Don’t say that! So what? You are going to be a monk for the rest of your life or something? Join the church then if you think relationships are bad. What the hell is Jesus talking about?” My heart was beating a million miles an hour at this point. There was definitely something different about my boyfriend. I could hear it in his voice. He was hesitant, in his head and unable to express what he was thinking – as though he had discovered the meaning of life and wasn't sure if anyone would believe him.

Ryan had become obsessive with reading other spiritual texts during our relationship and I didn't feel this book was going to be any different. *He will soon move onto something else* I comforted myself reassuringly after we had hung up and I had made him promise to not leave me. *I don't care who wrote that stupid book, even Jesus isn't going to persuade my Ryan that our relationship is unholy,* I reasoned. *How could that even be possible? We were on a mission for enlightenment together. Wasn't that holy enough?*

Although Ryan was undergoing a confusing spiritual period in his life, my spiritual dance workshops were thriving. I seemed to have the confidence to go into all areas of spirituality without much trepidation. I was teaching children's classes on psychic development. I held live shamanic music events where everyone could just come to dance. I led women's goddess circles out in my local forest. There was nothing I felt I couldn't do and I wasn't afraid of failure either. The things I was teaching held great meaning for me because I felt that they were what would bring me into contact with the Divine. As Ryan once told me, *if you want to learn something - teach it.* I didn't notice that he resented me for it until some months later.

I had a shamanic music band in to drum for a group of women I worked with. Ryan insisted on coming and stood, looking at the group of guys with suspicion, refusing to speak to them and leaving me bristling with anger. How dare he be rude to the people who were helping me! I wasn't paying them – they were doing the girl he loved a massive favor! He should at least be polite. I had honestly never seen him act like that before. But I brought my attention back to the group and left him alone in the kitchen space as he claimed he wanted to work on his laptop. I led a group meditation to relax us before we danced and noticed Ryan, peeping around the corner, not joining in like I thought he would.

"What's wrong with you tonight?" I asked, livid after everyone had left. He wouldn't answer for some time but eventually said,

"What you're doing is pointless. There is no point to it. Jesus in my book says that magic is wrong." Just when I thought I couldn't get any angrier with Ryan and his new best friend, Jesus, I did.

"So what are you? The Witchfinder general now?" I couldn't believe what I was hearing. "So… let me guess. I am going to hell because I worship Satan." Where had this sudden *fear* come from? We had been together for three years and he knew everything about me.

"I just think maybe you should change your ways or something. Magic is wrong." This wasn't the Ryan I knew – this was the Christian Ryan who was afraid of everything and I thought it was pathetic.

"Change my ways? You don't understand anything about what I do so how can you know if it is good or bad?" I shouted, losing my temper. "You have such a simple view of the world Ryan. After everything you have experienced I would have thought that you would be more open-minded. You knew I was a witch when you met me and *now* you are afraid? *Now*?" We grabbed our things and headed out on the ten-minute walk to the tube station. It was obvious there was something terribly wrong because we rarely argued, but neither of us were communicating efficiently enough to resolve it. I felt attacked for my beliefs and his silence was judgment enough. I didn't understand why our combined interest in spirituality had suddenly become the root of a major conflict in our relationship. Nothing between us after that workshop was ever quite the same.

There were a few times when Ryan would become angry at me for making him laugh or prompting him out of the 'character' he had built up for himself as a *spiritual guru* or a man on his way to enlightenment.

"Oh Tina!" He would say, disappointed. "People were saying I was different today… I was calmer and peaceful and now you are making me laugh! Stop!" I was amazed! He thought that when someone finally finds enlightenment it shows in how loud their voice is or how slowly they move?

"Don't be ridiculous! Enlightenment happens within you! You shouldn't be so eager to show every Tom, Dick and Harry how spiritual you are," I would retort, with my *Scott Cunningham* book in one hand and crescent moon ring on the other. Our belief systems were clashing big time and it had all started since I had given him *A Course in Miracles.* A terrible but subtle feeling that I was losing Ryan to it, swelled within me. How could he be so weak and at the same time egotistical to think that he would be able to live by those teachings? Those ridiculous, ideological teachings were for some sort of Utopian world; they were not for us, living in an ordinary borough of ordinary London. I began to hate Jesus and His incomprehensible words that preached against relationships and was stealing my boyfriend away from me. I wished with all my heart that I had never bought that horrible book.

Chapter 5

October 2007

I don't know the woman sitting on the end of my bed but I am adamant I am not dreaming. I am lying in the exact same position I fell asleep in. My view of the room is the same. There is no distortion on reality. I am moved more by my lack of fear than by fear itself, as I am overwhelmed with the knowledge I have known her forever. She looks down at me and the beauty and peace she exudes is infinite. Long, blonde hair shines like a cascade of stars down her back and her eyes glitter in different colors. Her head sways and shifts from left to right. On looking one way her eyes maintain a human appearance however when she looks back at me, they have grown in size – almost alien-like. In the midst of enjoying her presence, I suddenly hear a giggle and see my blankets moving to the right of me. Out pops the head of a little girl all blonde locks and blue eyes. She is laughing, the woman is smiling and I don't know why but I am weeping.

Never one to dismiss otherworldly experiences as wishful thinking, the next day, after I had written about the event in my pink satin dream diary that I religiously filled every morning, I called Ryan to tell him all about it. He was used to me rambling on about the occasional 'psychic' dream or some knock I had heard that I was convinced was a ghost trying to talk me. I could be a little dramatic at times.

"She was so beautiful Ryan! She was just sitting there looking at me! She had alien eyes and a child."

"Hmmmm… What did she say?" That's why I still loved him, tension aside. Four years into our relationship and he was *used* to me. I just told him an alien eyed woman had visited me in the night and he wanted to know if she had said anything. With a giggle I said,

"Nothing! She didn't have to." I lowered my voice and looked zestfully around my living room as though I were in a made-for-TV thriller. Grey walls and brown sofas stared back. "We spoke telepathically." I listened intently for his reaction to my exaggerated version of events. She actually hadn't said anything but what was wrong with embellishing the truth a little? It made life so much more exciting.

"Oh wow." He exclaimed with genuine enthusiasm. "I suspect she could have been an angel or something. Hang on a sec Tina. One of the girls is on the line." Ryan was at work and was probably concentrating on putting together a life-coaching session. That's what he had been focusing on that year. He taught people how to live their lives successfully and spiritually. He loved being able to help people because he had what he termed a 'Batman complex'. The desire to save anyone and everyone he came into contact with that gave even the slightest hint that they needed to be rescued. I admired this quality in him but it does have a downside in that it brings out the 'victim' in the people you love. Oftentimes I subconsciously took on the victim role in order to let him have the opportunity to play out what he thought was him in his natural, God-given state; The Superhero. I loved him and I wanted him to feel like he was fulfilling his life purpose so I played the victim of childhood memories, friends, as well as a couple of rogue managers of shady schools I got my first teaching jobs at and let him *save me*. Even his height and physique leant itself to convincing him that he was super-human. At 6'3 and obsessed with the gym, he would always be *Batman* to me but I figured he needed to hurry up and get back to the phone. A pang of jealousy came over me, wondering whom he was speaking to.

'One of the girls' he had referred to could either be Laura, Rianne or Deb. They worked with Ryan in his life-coaching company. I met them briefly once and they seemed okay if not slightly desperate somehow. At the time I didn't understand, but I too was soon to experience that same desperation. The same longing to have someone tell me the answers and to have someone confirm that I was special in some way.

“Hey I’m back – listen, we are putting together a gig for next Saturday. One group of teens I am mentoring has formed a band and wants to play at a pub in Greenwich. I want you to come. Everyone at my company will be there. Rianne and the others asked for you too.” My excitement at the possibility I had just met my guardian angel died with those words. In truth, I had been dreading this. Before this bloody life-coaching stuff had come along, Ryan and I had been inseparable. We took long walks by the Thames at midnight, fingers laced through fingers. We went to restaurants, just he and I. He could hang out with his friends whenever he liked but I had no desire to get involved with them. It seemed everything was changing.

“Ryan, you know I am going to say I don't want to. I have nothing in common with those girls. I won’t know what to say. They seem nice enough though, just not my type of people.” He took a deep breath and eventually said something that shocked me.

“If you don't start mixing with my friends, I am going to have to rethink our relationship.” I felt my face burning in anger. I have always been a shy, introverted person and being forced into social situations makes me uncomfortable.

“Why are you pressuring me into going when I have never been to any of your other events before? You weren't too bothered then!" A thick silence formed between us until I agreed to succumb to his wishes.

I had a strange feeling about his colleagues and I began to resent them over the coming week. They seemed to be building a wedge between Ryan and I. He was morphing into them; twenty-somethings, lured into the London lifestyle where only who you knew, what tube station you lived closest to and where you drank mattered. Deb wore a wool hat in summer and Rianne sat back to front on her chair. These girls were trendy and hip. In the ten minutes I had previously spent in their presence: the day I met them, I wanted to cry with the embarrassment of my long gypsy skirt and dangly earrings and tried to hide the ugly, vegetarian bag I was carrying.

"It's not like you're going to eat it!" My horrified, fashion conscious sister had said when I showed it to her in the shop. "Why don't you just get this *Mulberry* instead?"

Oh how I wished I had listened to her that day. I had been dancing in the forest behind my parents' home where I still lived that morning, and given a chakra-dance workshop in the afternoon. *I must smell of incense and musty, rained-on tree bark* I thought as I shook hands with the girls, one by one, projecting what I presumed was a cool breeziness but what must actually have been something more reminiscent of a moth realizing it had landed on a hot frying pan. I couldn't compete with them and their job contracts and rental agreements and woolen hats and plus, the thought of sitting in my chair like some kind of Neanderthal horrified me. The insecurities I had accumulated over the years were going off inside me like fireworks.

I looked up at Ryan and watched how he bantered with them and said witty things. Something had definitely changed. I knew his job with the media company had boosted his confidence and that his spiritual work made him feel like the next *Eckhart Tolle* but I didn't know what he would do to follow through with this make-over. Don't forget I was practically in competition with *Jesus* at this point and his annoying 'thou shalt not have a girlfriend' bullshit. I tried to push down that feeling of cold terror as I questioned whether, after all this, Ryan would still have room for me in his life.

When Saturday came I got on the tube to go to Greenwich. I had never been this far from home by myself. Except when I lived in Canterbury for university. Ryan usually went everywhere with me. I entered the old run down looking pub where the gig was to be held and made a beeline for the bar. I needed some wine. I stood alone, drink in hand and as the tinny music started up, I pretended to enjoy it. I could still feel my insides writhing around in anger at being forced to come to this pub by a group of girls who probably didn't even like me. I was also aware that I was angrier with myself for not enjoying social situations as much as everyone else my age seemed to. *Why didn't I fit in?* Maybe it was because I was the only witch in the room.

I watched Ryan out of the corner of my eye throughout the night, sauntering around as people approached him in reverence. *Fix me*, their faces seemed to implore. I observed him put his hand on shoulders, smile and lower his eyes in what I thought was a false display of humility. *He really is a guru now*, I noticed. He was teaching people about God and the universe and how to improve their lives and he, for some reason, was attempting to look and act the part. He was doing that slow-moving thing again. *Ugh!* I thought. *This is so stupid. His life isn't perfect... maybe he's teaching what he wants to learn?* I contemplated and sipped on the bitter drink in my hand. I did that too. I could relate to that. But I didn't understand why he had to wear his spiritual knowledge on his sleeve. I tutted and shook my head in annoyance, my crystal earrings tinkling as I moved, my seven pointed star bouncing on its chain against my chest. I watched, as he seemed to force a far away look in his eyes as if he imagined that was the gaze a spiritual guru might possess. I didn't get why he didn't want to laugh out loud and just *be himself.*

As the night wore on, I became more and more convinced that I didn't know this man. We were drifting apart. I was just tearing up at this awareness when a change came over the pub. Although crowded, it seemed to grow quieter and inexplicably, a space opened up on the large dance floor. I decided to look over my shoulder to work out what had happened. Someone was sitting on a stool there: just one person in this deserted clearing in this extremely busy pub. It seemed a light from above was shining down on her. It lit up her face in the darkness and I saw that it was one of Ryan's colleagues. It was Deb. I watched as her eyes moved from the stage to rest upon my own. As we locked gazes for that brief second, I can't explain how but I just *knew* that this girl was in love with my boyfriend and as someone very much ruled by my intuition, I accepted the inkling and let it swirl around me, breathing it in, trying to understand. The awareness that they were having sex settled among my thoughts. I realized he was her cult leader; her guru; her spiritual master and that to him, she was who *he* wanted to be. She had her own home, her own car and career. Everything Ryan didn't have yet but desperately wanted. Everything I didn't have but felt okay about. And that's where we differed. I couldn't follow him to that place of caring about money and status. I didn't know it yet, but he had already decided to leave me behind.

Chapter 6

Of course, I didn't confront Ryan about Deb. We didn't live together and so I had no evidence to prove that he was seeing someone else. I didn't notice any changes in his behavior or his daily routine and so I let things play out, all the while, hoping I was wrong. Ironically it was a night boasting a white, full moon that I discovered my intuition had been correct. The path of the Goddess teaches that the full moon grants wishes. I was sure I hadn't wished for this.

Almost a month had passed since the gig at the pub and on this dark blue evening, Ryan had requested that seeing as I was doing some shopping in the West End, I stop by his place in Victoria. I rang the doorbell with the strangest feeling of dread writhing around in my stomach. I watched as the door slowly opened. It didn't make a sound. In grey joggers and a T-shirt with the *Batman* symbol in yellow displayed front and center on it, he looked quite handsome. He had been going to the gym again and his upper body and shoulders were evident under the shirt. But when he looked into my eyes and sheepishly gazed at the floor, all of the muscle wasted away. The spiritual 'knowledge' drained from him in great puddles on the ground and the good standing he had built for himself with all of the people in his life collapsed in a heap. He looked so weak.

"Tina. I think we should break up. It's not you, it's me," he said, avoiding eye contact. I tried to take a deep breath but couldn't. My body was tensed, waiting to pounce on this man who said he wanted to marry me but who had obviously lied. He continued, "I'm having a spiritual crisis. I need to find God. The meaning of life."

I examined him in the darkness outside his front door and tried to think of ways to make things better. It was obvious that we barely knew each other at that point in time, but I didn't want to lose him. He was my life.

"Is there anything I can help you with…? What do you mean by spiritual crisis exactly? Is it… the book?" I saw that he had a familiar book in his hand. *Was he still reading A Course in Miracles?* I wondered. He saw me frowning at it and dashed it onto the floor. In a daze I followed it as it hit the ground in slow motion, its indigo cover falling heavily to one side revealing wafer thin pages. They looked frayed at the edges and torn, just like he did and I couldn't understand how things between us had deteriorated so fast. At the gig in Greenwich I had suspected that our relationship was going downhill but I didn't think for a second that he would actually want to let me go. Ryan shook his head then crumpled his nose like a three year old with a sniffle.

"That fucking book," he muttered. "I need time alone. Please don't call me again."

"What? Seriously?" I didn't know what else to say. I tried to remain calm and collected but my face betrayed me, eyes narrowed in distrust. This man seemed so weak to me now and he didn't want me to be witness to anymore of it. His body language was screaming at me to leave. His large frame blocked his doorway – the same doorway I had been welcomed through for so long. His arms were raised above his head and his fingers were locked on the little ledge above the doorframe, paling at the intensity of his grip. He needn't have bothered. I had no desire to enter his home. But I could see the harsh glow of the television in the background where his younger brother and sister were probably stretched out on sofas, oblivious to the scenario playing out on their front step. Ryan's little sister had become my little sister over the years and realizing I may never see her again, I bent my head and began to cry quietly so he wouldn't see my pain. He didn't deserve it.

"But what has brought this on? I cant believe you would call me all the way here just to listen to you lie. Just tell me who you are sleeping with." I said when I had gained my composure. He took a step back and in a sudden bolt of anger, I pushed forward. "It's Deb isn't it?" I wanted to lash out with fists or my tongue but his cold demeanor told me more than his words. He was saying I wasn't good enough. Not good enough to be with and not good enough to be owed an explanation. He whispered, glancing back at his siblings,

"There is nobody else involved. I just feel like I can't continue our relationship right now," and my reason for living was torn from me under a bright full moon.

Chapter 7

I was on my way to work when I got a phone call. I was startled by the shrill ring tone. The obnoxious noise drew attention on the quiet East London residential road. A church was coming up on my left. I walked past its ancient crumbly stone walls, digging in the black hole otherwise known as my bag. I fished around until I felt the cold metal and pressed the phone to my ear, reminding myself to change that bloody ringtone. I was taken aback when I heard the voice on the other end. Amelia - Ryan's sister. *Why was she calling me at quarter to nine on a weekday?* We exchanged awkward greetings. I was still headed to the college where I taught English but I slowed down my pace. My heart beat faster and I was instantly overwhelmed with a nausea that wouldn't leave me for the next two months.

"Listen. I need to tell you this. Yesterday, Ryan came over. He was driving a car I had never seen before." I felt my stomach drop. I knew what she was going to say. "It was a mini. He said it was Deb's."

I stopped dead, my tongue circling my teeth as I often did when I was fuming. Ignoring Amelia's cries to not tell her brother what she had just revealed to me, I hung up, ran the rest of the way to work, stormed into my manager's office and told him I was too sick to teach that day. He barely had a chance to reply before I was headed out the door on my way to the churchyard. It had the feel of being isolated although it was actually situated on a residential street. My fingers shook with an energetic anger, uncontrollable and fierce, but I managed to call his number. I heard his voice and then I heard what was supposed to be mine. But it didn't sound like me. Screams and cries that were enough to move the corpses in the graves scattered around me rung out loud and deep, as if they weren't coming from 'me' but from the deep dark depths of my soul. It felt wolf-like, wounded and feminine too, like the part of a woman that she has been taught to conceal her whole life. A dormant fragment carefully concealed within the spirit until she is so deeply wounded that she is compelled to let this new found energy arise until immersed in it. It surfaces to bellow out "this is not fair" and "I won't accept this anymore." I came to know her as my *primal self* and this experience brought me even closer to the Goddess in many ways. All my life, I had been known as the quiet one, the shy one, that girl who was too nice. Now here I was experiencing the hidden, darker depths of the Goddess rather than just reading about it and I finally knew there was more to Her than simply *love and light.*

I think a *primal self* is instinctive, intuitive, emotional, protective and loyal. She stands with matted hair falling over her forehead like a war helmet: taller, her heart large with true love and her belly swollen with beating life. Her forehead is wrinkled with lines of concern, each carefully defined and each representing a person she loves. She is the embodiment of love and yet she is the darkness that exists there too. When a woman is too fragile to cope with another stressor that life throws at her, primal woman takes the hit for her. When a woman swallows her sadness after another betrayal or loss, primal woman is drinking it in. This was the first of many encounters with this part of myself that seemed to exist within the abyss that is my soul. I didn't know her yet but what I discerned from her presence was that she resides in every woman; like a forgotten ancient secret, she sleeps until a woman who needs her strength wakes her.

I felt the words that left my lips that day, were the truest words I had ever spoken and yet the most untrue. Accusatory, derogatory words screamed into a telephone, and in the name of love?

"I hate you," I spat. "You're nothing but a loser." I was losing control of myself as I shouted out, "Who the fuck do you think you are?" and laughed maniacally, cruelly as I answered my own twisted question, "You're nobody. Tell your adoring fans the truth about you, Ryan. You are anything but *spiritual*. Spiritual people don't lie and cheat." My ugly tirade allowed no room for reply or reaction. After I had finished he said only one thing:

"You just verbalized my worst fears about myself."

That night he called me, resigned to the fact that not only had he been caught out but that he couldn't keep up his pretense of being a spiritual guru any longer. His voice was a whisper down the line as he said the words that made me feel so different and such an outcast.

"I'm afraid of you." I just waited and listened, too scared to speak. I had been caught out in my own small way. Primal woman had been frightening. "At the exact same time you called me this morning… I had to rush round to see the girls. Rianne said that she was paralyzed in her bed and that someone was slapping her. Tina. She could hear someone screaming at her that she was a bitch but there was nobody there." I swallowed, terrified at what Ryan was saying. I knew that his Christian upbringing would be kicking in right about now and that he was just as scared as me. "Laura said she dreamt of witches all night. And Deb. Well Deb's car has been written off. At the *exact same time* you screamed at me this morning, she drove straight into a lorry."

"Is she… okay?" I asked, concerned, not really knowing how this could have anything to do with me.

"Yes she is fine…. but Tina… They all went together to see a psychic who told them about you. The psychic guy said you weren't aware of doing it. It wasn't on purpose." I was annoyed. I hadn't done anything that I was aware of and to this day I don't know what to make of it, except that I have never been so hurt in my entire life as I was when primal woman came out. Ryan's call wasn't over yet though. He said, "I think you could kill everyone around me and leave me standing here."

I knew this was something he had been thinking about since he had confessed that he found my way of life wrong that day at my dance workshop. There was a rock solid certainty in his voice that stole my will to live because I thought he would never want to see me again. I believed he loved me but now he wanted to tell me that I was somebody to be afraid of. I almost broke my bed as I flung myself onto it and cried until my eyes stung. Why did life have to change so much. I wanted it to stay the same. *Why was the Goddess so unfair?*

The next few weeks I remember London covered in a dense, chilly fog that seemed to mirror everything I was feeling inside. I sure as hell had no idea whether I was coming or going and couldn't see where I was heading. I had never experienced a break down of a relationship in this way before. A man had never had to lie to me; had never chosen to sleep with someone else whilst they were seeing me. Not that I knew of anyway. I decided I had to forgive him. And then I thought I shouldn't forgive him and then I thought he should probably forgive me. And then I would have fleeting moments when I *remembered* him. I would pick up his picture and look in his puppy dog eyes. They went down at the corners. It made him look so pure and beautiful; as though the Goddess resided in there somewhere.

"No!" I would say and throw it roughly down onto the floor. I had expectations to fulfill; I had been cheated on and so I started to remember women from movies that had thrown themselves down onto their beds, face first, wailing in despair. And so I threw myself, face down onto my bed, wailing in despair. I remembered the people on nineties chat shows who would say "Drop that zero and get yourself a hero" and so I referred to him as a loser to all my friends and I had seen those women who search for themselves to escape a cheating husband and so I told everyone I was going to Glastonbury to *find myself*. Sometimes I recognized that my actions were the result of thoughts from the past: things I had heard, watched, read. But my vision was skewed and the more I focused on forgiveness, the more I focused on the thing he had done and pieces of my soul would fly away and dissolve into nothingness. I knew there was something wrong with how I was reacting to Ryan but I couldn't put my finger on it. I questioned whether what we are taught to believe about life and love was true. Was Ryan a bad person for sleeping with someone else? The more I looked down on him, the less I could face myself in the mirror. There had been so many times when I had looked this man in the eyes and seen myself. We were so close that there seemed no boundaries between his soul and mine, but he appeared to be at the stage in his life when that no longer mattered. He was strong in spirit but weak in the physical. He wanted money, power and recognition and he wanted it quickly, turning to a stranger in the hopes that by sleeping with her, he could take on what she had. He admitted that he was drawn to her for that reason. It was inevitable that he would end up leaving me behind. *Maybe*, I thought, *we choose people to have sex with based on who we want to be, thinking we can become them or own what they have in some form.*

I often considered the ethereal woman who had visited me at the end of my bed and strongly felt that *experience* was indicative of the upheaval I would face soon after. Was the encounter a calling to adopt a more spiritual stance to what was occurring? A Shamanic friend of mine suggested that she represented the divine mother energy because she had appeared with a child. We christened her 'Magda' and whether she was a dream, an angel or just an illusion, she became a symbol of comfort and hope for me in my darkest days and I couldn't see the wrong in that.

Chapter 8

I coped with the break-up by dancing like I had never danced before. I flung my shoes off, threw my arms up into the air and didn't care what happened next. I danced for freedom and so my feet chased wide-open spaces. The grasses of Wiltshire and Somerset in general were a favorite for me. I danced around Stonehenge and danced amongst the stones in Avebury with my mobile phone sounding out an Arabic belly dance from dewy grass. I would pack my little bag with clothes and candles and set off on my own adventure. When my feet couldn't dance anymore, I would settle under a wise papa Oak and write prayers and thoughts on parchment in Dragon’s blood ink. It was under such a tree in Wiltshire that I conceived the notion to marry *myself.*

When I first met Ryan, I had been experiencing a dark time in my life. I should have been socializing and enjoying London with my friends and family but instead I was a nervous wreck. I suffered from panic attacks to the point where I couldn't leave the house and I had a deep, ingrained fear of everything that had the potential to set my soul free. I would be somewhere as mundane as the tube and feel as though I couldn't breathe. The suffocating feeling haunted me, however Ryan was such a calming influence, and such a support to lean on that they stopped soon after I started spending more time with him. The result was that I leant on him too much – he spoke for me – he made me happy – he fought for me. I decided I had given too much of myself to this man. I had been open and vulnerable. *Yes that was it – that's why this has happened,* I thought. With determination etched into my face and heart, I promised I would never allow anyone the power to cause me pain again. And that's how I ended up in Glastonbury to perform a sacred marriage ceremony at the Chalice Well. I decided that I needed to stop relying on Ryan. I had to make vows to appreciate myself first: to look hard at myself, to know myself and 'love' whatever is reflected back in that mirror. What I didn't quite know was what it meant *to love.*

And so it happened to be at Imbolc that I arrived there at the hostel: a Pagan celebration of the end of winter and indicative of new beginnings and self-realization. I had travelled by coach that evening as I had never learnt to drive and no trains went to this isolated village town in Somerset. I saw the Tor from my coach window. It was the second time I had been there and both times it was an enchanting, awe-inspiring moment, to see that tall hill, reaching out of the ground towards the Heavens.

It turned out I was sharing my hostel room with a few other ladies who had come for the Imbolc celebrations at the Goddess temple that had been set up in the center of Glastonbury. A pretty place, it was a reasonably large workshop space that had beanbags on the floor and statues and paintings of the Goddess in her many guises on a vast altar. There was the Mother Goddess, the Maiden and the Crone. During Imbolc, they would put up an image of the Maiden – a representation of the pure, virginal, but adventurous young woman. I had been there before and enjoyed lighting a candle and saying a prayer. Above all though, it was nice to be amongst like-minded people who thought outside of the box and who approached their understanding of the Divine by placing equal importance on *experience* with it as opposed to merely blind belief.

So, waking up the next day, I marveled at the beauty of a frosty morning as I made my way through the streets of Glastonbury. When I got to the Chalice Well Gardens, the icy grass crackled as I lay down my scarf to use as a blanket. I was the only person there and all was as still as death. My frozen fingers held the little piece of paper upon which I had written vows to myself. The tealights I had placed beside me remained lit in the breezy air and seemed bright under the increasingly overcast sky. It had snowed in the night and there was a dusting of white over the fields beyond. I could see the hills over lumpy Somerset from where I was sitting. The tops looked like cupcakes dusted with icing sugar. I could feel magic in the air. There was a small waterfall cascading down a stoned wall in front of me, and I put my hand into it to feel the freshness and acknowledge my own connection to the element. Out loud, I read the vows, aiming for conviction in my voice. Voice was one thing though, my heart another.

"I promise I will love myself. I promise I will love the Goddess through me. Walk next to me my guardian angel, Magda. Walk with me Goddess in whatever is to come. I am strong. I promise my decisions will be wise and that I will turn my sadness into love for others for I understand that for others to love me, I must first know myself." Staring at the water falling in front of me, I vowed to become as fluid, flowing on and on, regardless of the jagged stones it encounters beneath it, water parts and comes back together again. I hoped my heart, although broken now, would find its way back together again.

Digging into my little satchel bag, I brought out the ring. I had taken ages to find it, eventually seeing it in the window of a used gold shop in an East London market. It was a nine carat gold band; antique, with a beautiful jade stone set in gold at the top. Fitting, as green is the color of love. I anointed it with water from the well and looked hard at it as though it were the antidote to a broken heart. My hopes and dreams were in that ring and they pretty much consisted of never being hurt again – an intention completely different from the purpose of the sacred marriage, which is to make vows that you respect and love yourself, ultimately entering into a spiritual contract between your mind, body and soul. The well-intentioned determination to focus on me was a fire that was licking at my insides and it suddenly felt angry. I had become disheartened with love and weary of men and their intentions. I swore I belonged to myself and thus, I wed myself there and then, slipping the ring on my wedding finger and possibly barred myself from ever feeling love again.

Chapter 9

January, 2008

"You're not going there," my dad said, with the force of a snapping turtle. But I wasn't asking if I could go, I was going and there was nothing anyone could say to change my mind. "You'll be kidnapped," he pressed, lips pursed, arms folded. I raised my eyebrows. "Seriously. It happens."

I had just heard that I would be going on a spiritual tour to Egypt and so I had informed my family. My dad wasn't afraid to voice his disapproval of my plans.

"I have to go." I said, refusing to budge. Bearing in mind what he had gone through in Turkey, unstable countries understandably made my dad anxious but I wasn't about to put my life on hold for what *may* happen.

The change in me since the breakup with Ryan had been profound. I was no longer scared and retiring, but desiring transformation in my life. I assumed the sacred marriage ceremony had worked and that it had given me the strength to rely solely on myself. I also knew that I wanted to live more than I wanted to remain fearful.

I turned my back on my dad and his negativity and headed upstairs to my bedroom to find my pictures of the Great pyramid and the Sphinx that I had enthusiastically cut out of 'National Geographic' many years ago. Even though I hadn't touched them for a year, I knew exactly where they were: white folder in the bottom draw of the large wooden chest to the right of my bed. I couldn't believe I now had the chance to go to this mysterious land I had been dreaming of for so long. I didn't know why but I had the urge to be free. I didn't know what I needed to be free from. I didn't know if it was Ryan. I didn't know if it was old memories. All I knew was that I needed to fly away: to leave my body behind in London and discover my spirit in Egypt.

I envisioned Egypt as a land littered with sacred sites where the Divine lived, possibly the Goddess, an energy ready to be tapped into by the average spiritual seeker. Maybe I would discover a past life or two. Maybe I would have a profound meeting with the Divine in its temple. I imagined myself asking it a dozen questions. Like why there is suffering in the world, why war exists and why Ryan thought Deb was better than me. I was still very much consumed by pain but I was prepared for my quest for the truth, even if the truth was something unexpected.

Chapter 10

The trip to Egypt was organized by a man who was well known in the UK for his work on Shamanism. It was to last for two weeks and in that time, it was planned that we would visit many sites from Cairo all the way down to Aswan. But as soon as the plane landed, I knew that my childhood dream would not play out the way I wanted it to. Maybe it was because I had come at the wrong time in my life. If I had wanted to be a tourist, I would have been satisfied beyond my wildest dreams; but I had come as a spiritual patient: a victim who needed healing. I didn't realize I wasn't the only one.

"Heather, Raven, Yiliz, Thomas…" We were still at Cairo airport and Bob, the organizer, was reading off his list of names to make sure nobody was missing before we queued for visas. Exhausted responses, some grumpy, others cheery, echoed out. *Hmmmm, a mixed bag*, I thought, looking around at twenty new faces. As he tried to get through his list, he was constantly interrupted by queries of the most irrelevant kind.

“Bob, can you tell me if you think I will be enlightened?” One man with very long hair and Jesus sandals was asking, poking and prodding at him like an annoying child.

“I think I am releasing… stuff,” said another who had just come out of the toilets in a jarring American accent. “I had diahorrea and I heard it means I am getting rid of the old to make way for the new in my life. That's right isn’t it Bob?”

“Oh yes,” he said. “That’s true. This trip will be important for you.” Diahorrea man sat down with an unnaturally white smile on his face. I had never seen anyone with a bowel problem look so pleased before. In fact I had never heard anyone so forthcoming about diahorrea before. A couple of people patted him on the arm as if to say, well done. “Tina… ah there you are,” Bob said, acknowledging me with the flick of his head. I had met him several times before. In fact it turned out that everyone on the tour had worked with Bob in some capacity prior to this trip. They may have gone to him for a psychic reading, or participated in one of his workshops on mediumship or shamanism. I had done both but I didn't know anyone else there. Ticking my name off his list, he looked back up at me and said, “This is Tina everyone. We were very close in a past life.” My heart just about jumped out of my chest. Feeling the immediate change in atmosphere I later thought I would have done better to dash outside onto one of the giant tarmac runways and get crushed by a plane wheel. I was now facing the wrath of twenty other spiritually needy people. Executed like a composer silencing an orchestra, Bob's words killed all questions, all conversation and almost all movement. Just a lot of eyes glaring at me now, it was a terrible introduction to the rest of the group who would have done anything for Bob's attention. *Why did he have to do that?* I thought, cringing inside.

Arriving at the hotel in Cairo was unreal. We could see the pyramids from the hotel grounds and I couldn't believe it. They stood out, ancient and proud in a swirl of dust and sand and it was like a dream come true. Looking at the desert in the distance, was better than seeing it in the pages of a magazine. In fact it felt so unreal, finally achieving this dream of mine to see Egypt that I felt myself becoming ungrounded. This can happen, for instance, when a psychic does a reading and doesn't meditate afterwards, to close himself off from the energy fields he had exposed himself to during the reading. It's sort of like, feeling too many emotions at once, most of which do not belong to you. Bob noticed I was struggling and called out for someone in the group to help. I felt embarrassed to behave like a needy spiritual person, but I really was feeling strange and I hoped I wasn't having a panic attack. I hadn't had one of those for years but the terror that they might come back again has always followed me and probably always will.

A pretty girl with long red hair and dressed in a gypsy skirt, scarves, crystals and feathers came flouncing out of nowhere and led me to a hotel room. She introduced herself as Sian and said we would be roommates.

"Lie down on the floor so that you're on something steady. We need to get you feeling grounded again."

"I know," I said between long gulps of air, "it happens to me all the bloody time."

"You poor thing." She said sincerely. Her accent was posh and had a slight West-country tinge to it.

"You from Devon then?" I asked, curious.

"Yep! I have a crystal business and I am an artist." There was a pause as she placed a reddish crystal at my feet. I was starting to relax. "This is so exciting to be here isn't it," Sian went on. "I've never been to Egypt before. And isn't Bob great? He's amazing. I met him at a show years ago and I have been going to his workshops ever since." I thought again about Bob and how everyone had been reacting to him. I was a follower of his work and had been personally involved in the new age movement through my London based workshops for many years, but my shy streak kept me from throwing myself at his feet like some of the other people were, although, I wanted to. I wanted to break down and cry and hear his comforting words. He had the answers. I was sure he had the answers. Yes, I was more independent now, but I needed to find myself, and who better to do that for me than a spiritually powerful teacher.

Sian was putting some brown crystals on my legs and waving her arms about. Whenever I got ungrounded, it would feel a bit like shortness of breath and I would get pins and needles in odd places like my head. Whatever she was doing it was helping. After some time I hauled myself up and looked into the mirror to re-do my curly ponytail that had come loose from lying down.

"Thanks so much, I feel much better now. I think they may have brought our luggage to our door. Shall we get settled and then Bob will want us downstairs for dinner at eight."

She nodded in agreement as she opened the door and pointed to our cases that had been piled up outside.

Dinner turned out to be torturous.

"I think I have had eight past lives here." Said one woman dressed all in purple.

"Only eight?" said another. "I have had at least fifteen."

"My hypnotist said I was the personal high priestess of Isis. I can't wait until we go to the Isis temple on Wednesday! I am sure I will remember so much! I'm bound to really!" People were reaching over each other for salad and chips but all rustling stopped when Bob spoke.

"Yes," he said confidently and with a laugh. "You will all be discovering the many past lives you have had here on this sacred land." Eyes widened around the table. Bob would know what they were.

"I am sure I was a high priest in the Valley of the Kings and Queens before." A woman dressed all in blue, said as though she were asking a question. Bob got it, nodded affirmatively at her and her face lit up. Then Bob looked at me and I felt my face ignite. Again he made a point of saying,

"Tina was my daughter in a past life."

Everyone shifted to look at me. I stared back like, *that's news to me* but to my amazement, no one noticed and people began asking him if I had been their daughter, little sister and granddaughter. Although I felt awkward, due to stealing focus, I couldn't help but enjoy the moment and take it to mean that he was seeing something in me that the others didn't have. I smiled good-naturedly at everyone and made surprised humming noises at them, bobbing my head up and down vigorously and widening my eyes to show I had no idea that the person across from me had been my mother four hundred years ago in some city someplace. I wanted to appear humble. *I must be different from them* I thought. *If they want to claim me, it must be because I am spiritually better in some way.*

It turned out that Bob was related to Cleopatra, another woman was Queen Hatshepsut and a rather retiring looking man was Ramses the second. As everyone got back to eating after the excitement had passed, I was secretly disappointed that I was no longer the center of attention. I was generally a shy person and so that took me by surprise. I needn't have worried though because my moment in the spotlight wasn't over yet.

"If this were forty years ago, I would have been dying to be you." Everyone went quiet as the munching of falafel sandwiches ceased mid-chew. Ten pairs of eyes at my end of the long pull out table were on the woman who had spoken. The other end of the table where Bob was sitting was oblivious. They were having their own conversation about past lives. "Yes. I would have wished I was you, but now I have learnt to relish my own power." It was an older lady who had spoken, probably in her seventies. She was stunningly beautiful, with clear blue eyes and a mop of bright pink hair. It was cut stylishly in a pixie look and her face was made up in subtlety that matched her skin tones and brought out her eyes. Yes, her face was lined in wrinkles – the good fight that told a story of love, love and more love – but it only made her incredibly dignified and elegant. I would have smiled at her and continued making my falafel sandwich if this woman hadn't been looking directly at me. *Oh my Goddess*, I thought. *Is she talking to me?* Apparently she was because now everyone was also looking at this girl who had so far, not spoken a word. I had just been nodding away like a toy dog in a car's rear window. *They must think me so stuck up* I thought. *I had better say something.*

"Why?" I croaked. It was all I could muster what with the embarrassment and all.

"I always wanted to have your power when I was your age. I just didn't know I already had it." She paused. Her face was deadly serious and now I was mortified but I tried to maintain control of my expressive eyes. I didn't want to embarrass her.

The people around the table were staring at me – some were amazed and some filled with pure spite. The truth was that they were all there to be recognized. They wanted to be special somehow. I did too, because I wanted a reason for why I had to start my life again and without the man whom I had planned to marry and father my children. Had the Goddess intervened and split us up and if so why? Did I have another calling? It was only natural to ask these questions if one was spiritually inclined. All these people had been asking some version of that question too. "You have a lot of power." She nodded and continued eating her chips, all the while gazing at me as though she could see something that I couldn't see. I didn't have a clue what to say in response; all I knew was that there were still a lot of people staring at me. When they realized I wasn't going to say anything more, they began whispering amongst themselves, pink-haired woman going back to eating as though nothing had transpired between us.

Chapter 11

The next evening, Bob, with his connections had managed to secure private time in the Ramses pyramid in Giza thanks to a man named Yamen. He was a very open minded Egyptian who had the job of over-seeing the smooth running of various spiritual tours. I liked his eyes. They were a watery yellow and stood out against his dark, tanned skin. I felt as though I were looking into the eyes of his ancestors. They seemed to hold so many secrets; secrets that had drawn me to Egypt since I was that teenager tearing pictures of the pyramids out of magazines.

Entering the Great pyramid was suffocating as there was only a tiny corridor leading downwards and on deciding to go down, there was no way to turn and go back unless you reached the bottom first. I was grateful we had private time because I couldn't imagine how horrible it must be with hundreds of tourists squashed together in that tunnel, like London underground commuters at rush hour.

As I got to the end, only a sarcophagus sat to one side of the inner pyramid. There was nothing else inside. The walls were bare and a faded sandy yellow. Everyone was laying their bright scarves on the floor and sitting down. I waved my hand in front of my face trying to get some air - it was really humid in there. Bob and a few of the other people were preparing their drums; the Shamanic kind that are beaten with a stick and made of goatskin. I enjoyed the sound they made and was looking forward to hearing their collective beat. Yamen made his way back to the outside entrance to the pyramid and turned off the electricity supply. We were thrown into a pure blackness. There was silence and the dark was so thick, I felt as though I were breathing it in. I was startled when someone's stick struck their drum and the others followed.

There was a lot of wonderful music played and songs sung but I didn't feel much. It felt bland inside this mythic structure and yet Bob had said how he had encountered strong forces and energies that had propelled him into enlightenment. He had said it would heal, but I felt nothing. When we boarded the bus to go to the next sacred site in Cairo, everyone was raving about the things they had experienced.

"I feel refreshed!" said the blue woman.

"I have been there before in another life!" exclaimed another wildly excitable woman with tears streaming down her face. I stared at her and furrowed my brow in contemplation for a second before turning to Sian. I didn't want her to think I was an unfeeling moron.

"I didn't really get anything from there" I whispered. Sian *was* 'floaty' but definitely had her down to Earth side.

"I just liked the drumming a lot but I did feel a lot of energy," said Sian in between gulps of water. I watched her saunter away and mingle with some other people from the group and smiled at the glimpses I caught of her trademark colorful stripy socks under her gypsy skirt.

As we boarded the coach again, I realized in excitement that we would need to drive back to the hotel through the desert. I was getting into the habit of practically pressing my nose right up against the coach window lest I should miss a mountain, or a Bedouin camp or a rock in the desert. Being my first time in the Middle East (except Turkey, where I spent a lot of time as a child) I had concluded it was everything I had imagined it to be. The dusty mountains were so mighty and seemed to throb with magnificence and power. I thought I caught glimpses of life moving inside them and if I looked hard enough, one might lift up a heavy foot out of the Earth and make a step toward me. The Egyptian landscape moved me more than the pyramid had. I wasn't sure if that was a good or bad thing in terms of 'being spiritual'. I looked around at the other people on the coach who were hugging each other and still lightly drumming out the songs they had played earlier. Was I the only one not to sense energies? But Bob had suggested I was different from everyone else. I was supposed to be his ‘daughter’. I should have been the one to have some kind of transcendent experience. Despite my concerns, I eventually let my mind wander back to the dinner when pink-haired lady had said I was ‘powerful’ and I straightened my back to sit higher than everyone else in my cramped coach seat.

Chapter 12

"Are we ready everyone?" Bob was speaking and twenty eager faces looked up. With irritation they reminded me of Ryan's 'followers' so I looked down to rummage through my bag. I didn't want to appear as desperate as they did, although I felt it. The Great pyramid hadn't given me any insight into who I was and time was running out. "We are heading to Dendera. It is the best, preserved complex of temples in Egypt and consists of an Isis temple, a sacred lake and the main Hathor temple to name but a few of the Roman inspired architecture. Now a few of you, I know will experience past life flashbacks. Might I suggest you take time to connect to your spirit guides now so that you are more open to the energy." Everyone ooo-ed and ahhh-ed and as the wheels of the coach started rolling, I looked up to find several people making a weird humming sound. They were holding enormous quartz crystals and a guy I took to calling 'open-toe sandal man' because I could never remember the name he insisted we call him (something like John raven-wing, eagle-body), sounded like he was trying to invoke the Goddess Hathor. Sian and I made eye contact across the aisle and tried not to laugh.

Dendera turned out to be one of the best experiences I have ever had. I explored it alone and it just felt so feminine that I found myself moving sensually between the great structures. My hands clasped each pillar as I flowed through them and I took off my shoes to feel the sand under my feet. I looked around me to see oceans of desert blowing up, disturbed by minute gusts of wind. Then I noticed my shadow on the floor, cast behind me, elongated and graceful. I stretched out an arm and saw how my fingers delicately formed shapes on the sand. I stretched out a leg and pointed my toes, the movement so fluid and elegant. I did it again and again, never taking my eyes off my shadow until I realized I was dancing. There was no music playing but I was moving with my shadow in this beautiful place where the Goddess was worshipped and the divine feminine had a place in Heaven. Hathor was the Goddess of joy and music, motherhood and love. Somehow, everything the people on the tour had spoken of was making sense. There did seem to be traces of energies drifting in the air around these temples but whether I had brought the energy or whether it resided there, created by the temple, I didn't know. I kept moving and dancing to the music of Hathor until I forgot I had a body. All I could see was my shadow and it felt like she was giving power to my spirit. The truth of what I was. I was spirit. I danced for eternity until tourists were taking pictures of me and a group had gathered to watch. A few Egyptian men armed with drums and traditional instruments appeared from nowhere and played a haunting tune and women started to join in. The music played and we all danced until the sun had set and I could no longer see my spirit.

Scrambling into bed that night, Sian and I giggled about our day and relayed the experiences we had had in Dendera.

"Bob was giving us private readings in the main temple. It was great fun." Sian said, clambering into bed. "He said Lizzy and I had been sisters and that Graham should stay on in Egypt for a while."

"Really?" I asked. "I was thinking of doing that too. I think I might."

"Oh I wish I could stay with you but I have work to see to." I was disappointed. I had grown quite attached to this fascinating lady who was so true to herself and had no concern for the opinions of others. I wished I were more like her. She continued, "Bob keeps calling you his daughter."

Bob *had* taken to referring to me as his daughter in front of the group and I would feel poker red eyes burning the top of my head, as I looked at the floor in awkward silence. Then he would ask me if I felt anything in the temples we visited and most of the time I would have to say no, whilst other group members were eager to share their feelings.

"Yes, I am not sure how I feel about that. It's getting a bit embarrassing." I told her, cringing. It made me feel important, yes, but I almost wished he would do it privately, between us – our secret. It was affecting my friendships with others in the group. "I wonder if he's doing it on purpose." I muttered under my breath.

"What? No way Tina." Sian assumed I meant that he was trying to embarrass me but I was referring to an attempt to isolate me from everyone else.

"To be honest, I am not really *feeling* much – or as much as everyone else it seems. It just seems a bit silly to single me out in that way. Why not single out Christina? She was rolling around on the floor the other day – *releasing stuff* – remember? She was channeling something I guess. Christina is a much more likely candidate for role of daughter."

I hid under my blankets, not wanting to hear what Sian was saying. Dendera had been amazing but I still felt the same. I hadn't been transformed yet. I thought about how I had wanted to be healed before I came to Egypt, and how only the nature seemed to interest me. The temples were not instigators of enlightenment after all, but hollow shells devoid of power for spiritual transformation. I understood that now.

A few more days into the trip and I was convinced that instead of healing I had stumbled upon a great ancient war that was similar to the war playing out inside of me; where the deserts became great battlefields of a fight between the Goddess and man. I was in awe of the mountains that stood strong and proud; after all it was they who had been created by the divine hand of mother Earth. I looked up in wonder at great temples that seemingly had life-blood flowing through them. Their pillars like great giant roots, twisting and swirling under the surface, sucking up the admiration of all who came to see them and feeding off of those people who had unwittingly become a kind of sacrifice. In return for their wonder, they had given great meaning to these man made structures. But the Goddess didn't live there. I slowly came to realize that I had come to this country, hoping the temples and their ghosts would see me and bless me and release me of everything I had done wrong with Ryan. The reality of what I was hoping would change me hit me hard. *Temples and ghosts.* How could something so man-made be expected to reach my soul?

One day David saddled up to me as I had my nose pressed to the window on another long bus journey between sacred sites. David was a sour faced man who didn't say much. He was the husband of one of the organizers and had obviously not chosen to be there of his own accord. He and his wife were having marital issues and I wanted to stay out of it. I couldn't really imagine what I would have to say to him anyway. He was twice my age and he wasn't looking for anything out there in the Egyptian desert. He wasn't wearing crystals or saying anything that indicated that he believed in the magic of the land. I wasn't interested in him but he seemed to have something to say to me.

“You think you’re special. You’re not special.” I slowly inch away from the window and do a one-eighty in my cramped seat. David is sitting next to me.

"Excuse me?" I say, my face a picture of disgust that someone would come from nowhere and start throwing insults around. I look him up and down and a flash of gold catches my eye, a glittering star on a chunky, indigo blue book resting in his hands. *I've seen that book somewhere before.* Amidst this flash of instant anger I can't remember where.

"You heard me." He says simply. "Stop acting like all the others. They think they're special too."

"What do you mean though? How do we think we're special?" I almost shout back.

He is looking in my direction but his deep, glassy eyes never seem to catch mine. They are aimed *past* me and I experience a brief moment of fear. He looks like a madman.

"You want something on this trip to tell you that you are special or different but we are all the same under God." He says, fingers tapping lightly on the cover of that mysterious book. I am taken aback. This man is being so direct with me. His face is straight as an arrow. He isn't trying to sugar coat his accusation. It is what it is. And what does he mean by God? This isn't a Christian gathering. *Is that a Bible in his hands? Is he trying to convert me?* "Be aware," he continues. "Haven't you noticed how these people are trying to put you down?"

"I don't understand," I mutter. My eyes must have been blazing with fury at this point. You can take the girl out of East London but you can't take East London out of the girl.

"You haven't realized that you are always the daughter, the little sister, the priestess or the princess?" I can only look stupidly at him as the events of the trip so far come flooding back to me. "That's what it takes to become special. Someone always has to be less in some way. You are no less than Bob. You can do everything he can. You are a high priestess. You are a queen." I had heard that David was a miserable bastard but his words weren't matching the expectation and I am caught off-guard. *Silence*. I literally have no words. I notice most people have fallen asleep. The soft sound of breathing is all I can hear. And the tapping.

"Actually" I finally say, "You are so right! This hasn't felt right to me. This isn't right."

I can only stare at him in awe. My mouth is suddenly drying up. Maybe it's because I have left it open like a fish.

"Hold onto your truth. You lost it all because you wanted to feel special. You were enjoying being Bob's daughter and in that enjoyment you forgot who you were."

"But who am I?" I whisper desperately.

"Priestess, witch, queen, commander of the elements. Whichever pointless title you give yourself if you want me to say what you want to hear that is. However, if you want the truth: if you want to live a life of peace, I would say that you and I and everyone here are children of God. Never can there be peace among the different."

I couldn't believe it. I had come all the way to Egypt to find myself in a dilapidated remnant of events passed when all I had to do was go to Bristol to have a chat with David.

Throughout the rest of the tour he never engaged me in friendly banter about the weather or a past life but he made me question every word I allowed to pass my lips with a stern face. He made me question the motives behind what I said and it kept me on my toes and in a state of heightened awareness. Once, I announced to Sian and Bob that I felt travelsick. He breezed through the coach aisle and up to me with my hands pressed against my stomach and whispered,

"Stop trying to be special." I looked at him, annoyed but let go of my belly and sat up straight. I had no clue what he meant but I wanted to – he was gone before I could say a word.

He also watched my reaction carefully when I was asked to join a spiritual naming ceremony to be performed by Bob. The purpose of it was to have Bob use his psychic knowledge to give everyone a new, 'magical' name. I could feel David's eyes resting on me from a distance and I knew I was supposed to refuse. I tried to understand why he might think participating in the naming ceremony was wrong. *My name is Tina. I do not need Bob to name me and just the intention to have him do so is a poorly disguised hope that he will give me a name that will make me feel special or better than someone else. It will give him a power over me.*

I could see Bob's irritated face glaring at me a little way away as he instructed the group to sit in a circle on the desert floor. He had obviously wanted to *name me*. Alone, I sat on my sandy rock, hypnotized by several colored scarves trying to get away from their owners to dance with the wind. I had been trying not to but curiosity got the better of me and I looked up to see David standing on a crumbling wall. For the first time on the trip, he smiled at me.

Chapter 13

Betty, a beautiful, gentle soul had twisted her ankle so I went to visit her in her hotel room dragging Sian along with me. As we talked, Sian settled in an old-fashioned chair and I sat on the floor. A few other ladies from the trip bundled in too and we had a fun time, laughing and gossiping. I was fiddling with my turquoise crystal necklace when Sian complimented it and I looked up to thank her but something wasn't right. She was there but what I can only describe as a mist was swirling around her. To date, it is still the most bizarre thing I have ever seen.

I tried blinking a few times, closed my eyes and opened them again but no! It was still there, engulfing my friend until all I could see was her face. Although it wasn't her – it was someone else sitting there now. An older woman upright in the armchair with similar features - a pale complexion, yet her hair was redder, thinner and wilder. Grey weaved its way through and there were heavy wrinkles in her face. Her clothes were different too. Now she was wearing a dirty, torn, white smock type dress. All I could think of to say was,

"Have you ever been interested in the days of Robin Hood? Did you ever feel a connection to that time period because right now I am seeing you, looking exactly like a character from Sherwood Forest!" We had only met a week and a half ago and were totally immersed in all things Egyptian. Nobody was thinking of Nottingham, back home! Her eyes lit up as she slowly said,

"Yeeees." Her tone suggested that she was surprised I had known that. Heck, I was surprised I had known that but I realized my mistake immediately as I turned to look at the rest of the room. I shouldn't have announced it out loud. Betty was smiling at me but the other women's faces were cold. I recognized that hardened glare from the last couple of months of my relationship with Ryan. A mixture of jealousy possibly with a massive dose of fear and I was very disappointed. Yes, I was a desperate spiritual patient here in Egypt, but I wasn't in competition with anyone. I didn't care who could sense the most past lives or who would be the next *Bob*. I didn't give a damn and I wasn't even sure I believed in reincarnation anymore. All I wanted was to feel whole again and to understand why my life had turned out the way it had.

At dinner, I made sure Sian and I grabbed seats near to David so that he might overhear our conversation. I needed his help yet I was too afraid to approach him because every time I made anything into an issue, he would simply say I was looking to be *special* not to mention the fact that he always looked so strict.

"Why are you shouting, Tina? I have a pounding headache," said Sian, looking more amused than annoyed. I tried not to burst into giggles,

"Shhhh … I want David over there, to hear me, that's why!" I whispered, glancing around to make sure he hadn't heard. "I haven't read that bloody book of his, in fact I haven't even seen the front cover. I think I've seen it before but I'm not sure. He keeps acting like I have read it and … using terms from it that I am not familiar with. I just need his help... to understand. Play along." Sian looked highly tickled now as I raised my voice above the clanging and the voices in the restaurant. "I don't think the energy of Egypt is working for me. I need more! I wish *someone* would advise me on what to do. I really need healing."

"He's not looking. I don't think he heard you." Sian mouthed in an exaggerated whisper and we both tried to stifle our laughter until we cried.

I was convinced David hadn't heard my 'subtle' plea for spiritual help but it turned out I was wrong. It finally occurred to me how I knew the book David carried everywhere with him – the indigo one I had seen in his hands on the coach on the first day he confronted me. It was the same book that had destroyed my relationship with Ryan. I knew it now because it was lying on the floor outside my hotel room door.

"Ugh!" I sighed out loud as I picked it up roughly, carried it into my room and threw it onto the floor. "What do you want from me?" I examined it in the light of a bedside lamp. David's copy no doubt. I traced my finger over the gold writing on the cover, *A Course in Miracles, Foundation for Inner Peace…*

Even though I had been very drawn to David's words and way of looking at the meaning of life, knowing that it had come from that book – the same one that Ryan had used against me – I just couldn't get over it. I remembered how Ryan had said that the book contained the words of Jesus and to me that was an excuse to dismiss it as Biblical nonsense that was out to kill my divine feminine. *There*, I thought *if anyone asks why I haven't read it that will be my reason. I am a witch and witches are different. We don't take our orders from books written by the divine rather we create our own books with the spirit of the divine flowing through us.*

Chapter 14

I didn't return to England with the rest of Bob's group much to the dismay of my family back home. Instead, I tore up my return ticket and chucked it in the bin. I wasn't ready to give up on Egypt yet. I decided to live in Luxor, home of the Valley of the Kings and Queens, in case I wanted to give the possibility of being healed by the temples another go.

I tried to further help my healing along by working with the poverty stricken street women whom I decided to teach English to, in the hopes that they would be able to interact more with foreigners and be more effective at selling their wares. I rented a flat especially for female expats and worked on my project for a couple of weeks before discovering that living in Egypt alone as a single British woman was a terrible idea and I don't think I could have been further from spiritual if I had tried. *Fuck off* was as commonplace is my vocabulary as *hello*.

Firstly I noticed very little numbers of Egyptian females actually walk the streets so when I did, I may as well have had a neon sign flashing 'foreigner' fixed to my forehead. I couldn't walk down the road without comments from pervy men or gangs of children poking and prodding me like a dying coal fire. It confined me to walking down one or two roads I knew well to get places. Secondly I became afraid to leave my flat because the caretaker of my building – a middle-aged Nubian man with elongated arms and legs and shiny black skin, was convinced that because I was a Western woman I would want to have sex with him. The guy lived in a bizarre cage-like contraption under the apartment block staircase and probably had a bath once a month. I can safely say that I did not want to sleep with him. But he continued to harass me which included forcing himself into my flat, sitting on the sofa and switching on 'Egyptian porn' (which was actually a kissing scene from a Hollywood movie) and masturbating. My heart would beat a million miles an hour when he would knock on my door in the early hours of the morning, trying to get in. He knew I was home and he could sometimes wait outside for me for up to thirty minutes, knocking over and over again, which terrified me.

One night he entered my flat just as a friend (a guy who also knew the caretaker) had left and the door was still open. He closed and locked it behind him. He was holding a small tray with a large glass on it. I could see steam coming off of the orangey looking fluid. I saw it rise up like a snake from a basket and I watched it in a trance. I wanted to be anywhere but there but I couldn't move with fear.

"Sick, sick" was all he could muster in English, whilst pointing at my stomach and shoving the tray in my direction.

I had been ill for several days with food poisoning. I didn't know how he knew that. I managed to focus on him and take the glass because I didn't know what else to do. A lemon fragrance wafted out of the glass and in my face. The smell of it aggravated the newfound nausea, swirling around in my stomach. My hand shook as I tried to smile. *Maybe he will go now* I thought as desperation to flee was creeping up on me. Then he was pointing to my bed and I thought my stomach was in my mouth. It was hard to separate the thoughts that were racing through my mind at that moment because logic took over. I was starting to understand how Arab society worked from the bits and pieces I had picked up from several Egyptian friends I had made and that knowledge was at the forefront of my mind. I remember thinking that he would know the consequences of his actions. He knew that crimes against foreigners would be dealt with more harshly than those involving locals. He knew he would probably lose his job and home. He took a step toward me. He had an expectant look on his face, as he looked me up and down – as if he was waiting for me to rip my clothes off in a sex-crazed frenzy. He took another one, impelling me backwards into my bedroom and carefully taking the glass out of my hands to put it on the floor. He was positively beaming with glee. He was sure he was going to have sex and what really bothered me was that I knew that he thought I *wanted* it. As though the very air I breathed was sex and that it kept me alive.

I am British after all – I realized I was lower than low to him at that moment and that my body was not sacred because he *believed* it had engaged in sex out of wedlock – just like those women in the Hollywood movies he watched and masturbated over. I was less than human. I was a woman whose worth was measured in the pleasure I could give to a man. My eyes darted around the room but there was no way out. He was six foot two at least, and had done physical work his entire life – you could see it sculptured into his frame. I became very present as he made me sit on the bed and then put his entire body weight on me to force me in a lying position. I was suffocating underneath him as he put his elbow into my neck and his legs across my knees. I couldn't breathe with the smell: sweat combined with soap on his hands. *He must have just been praying*. The thought babbled through my mind like someone had left the tap on. What a strange thing to think about at a time like that. Inwardly, I called out for

Ryan and then Magda and the Goddess to help me interspersed between attempts to take a breath when, without warning he slid to the ground next to the bed and gazed down at me with a smirk on his face. It was as though I belonged to him – I was his prized possession as he put his soapy-smelling hand out to stroke my hair. I tried to get back up again but I found that my body felt locked – like my muscles were tensed waiting for the right moment to leap into action. I felt like a cat, waiting to be pushed into going for the kill. I wanted to kill him: to rip his eyes out.

I barely breathed as his hands lifted up my jumper and started touching my stomach. *How did I get myself into this?* I thought. I didn't want to look but I couldn't close my eyes. Then, in an instant, a way out of this situation came to me like my prayers had been answered. I realized I might be able to play on the sensitivities of the Egyptian culture. Immediately, I grabbed for my phone, pointed at it and said the word *uncle* in Arabic. I breathed out in relief as I saw the recognition in his eyes. I watched him closely to see what he would do, still ready to pounce. I could see he was weighing up the pros and cons. After what felt like hours but was in reality a few seconds, he got to his feet, a skyscraper lingering above me, still helpless on my bed. But I knew. I knew he was deathly afraid that I would tell our mutual 'friend' about what he was about to do to me. He hadn't considered it before but the reality hit him now and I watched in disbelief as he walked out of my flat without saying a word. And that was that. It was over.

Sadly, I was too frightened to tell anyone what was happening. I eventually became so ashamed of my inability to speak up I fled Luxor on the train and headed for Giza where I stayed with a friend of a friend and his wife and baby. Foreigners are not allowed to travel on the overnight train I took but I disguised myself – not that hard to do as I have dark hair, hazel eyes and Turkish features – by slipping a headscarf on and avoiding eye contact at all times. I felt annoyed for having to abandon my project with the street women and not following through with all the spiritual things I had wanted to do like visit more temples, but I just didn't feel safe alone there anymore.

In my sleepy haze, early the next morning, I remember getting caught once I arrived in Cairo, but a man on the train helped me get out of it somehow. I didn't understand what was going on as they were conversing in Arabic. My clearest memory though, was wishing the whole ride across country, that Ryan had been there to protect me when the caretaker was making my life a living hell. I needed my Batman for real now but he wasn't around.

Chapter 15

My heart raced with excitement upon reading an email from a guy called Pete, confirming an offer of a position as English teacher at a British run school in Damascus, Syria. I wrote back,

Dear Pete

Thank you for your email. I would be delighted to accept the role of English teacher at the British School, Damascus, for the summer program. Is it possible for you to confirm the date I will be flying out?

Kind regards,

Tina

I hit 'send' and waited. Doing a three - month summer school wasn't ideal as I would have preferred an annual, full-length, full-time contract but I supposed it was better than nothing. I had seriously been applying for ages now and no suitable opportunities had arisen. I was lucky to get it. I thought it might at least look good on my CV.

An hour later I checked my inbox again and found an email from Pete. I was completely baffled. It read,

Dear Tina

I think there's been some mistake. This job is a full time, two - year

contract. We haven't even advertised our summer school vacancies yet. Knowing this, are you still willing to accept the position?

Pete

I couldn't believe my eyes. Looking back at the paperwork I had, it was there in black and white: *summer school contract: July to August.* I thought it best not to pursue it with Pete as he was to be my manager yet I was more than a little freaked out mainly because I probably wouldn't have applied for a contract that lasted so long – a year is long enough, but two? After all, this was new to me. Going on holiday and deciding to stay was different to flying out for the purpose of moving and working. There would be boxes to ship and people to say goodbye to that I wouldn't see for about six months. But I didn't have time to be overwhelmed. I had a job to accept and a new life to embrace; no doubt the Divine felt the need for some serious intervention here because how I ended up living in Syria for two years is unexplainable. As I got to know Pete, we would bring it up sometimes and neither of us could figure out how it happened. The interview had been more than an hour long so surely the contract length and role would have been discussed. It still baffles me now.

I had applied for this job on my return to England. I lasted, in total, about five months in Egypt alone, two of which were spent with a lovely family who took care of me in Giza. I taught them English and I learnt some Arabic and best of all, my bedroom's balcony looked out toward the great pyramid, the Sphinx, not to mention the vast desert. My national geographic pictures had come to life! If I looked down to the streets below, young men were camel racing and if I turned down the television at eight o'clock, I could catch the nightly light show (I lived *that* close) – blue and purple beams brought the pyramid to life. I could hear the story of those wondrous structures booming out across the desert where I caught glimpses of tourists on horses, disappearing into early morning mists that loved to settle over the desert. Overall, I was relaxed and felt safe with the family at their house but I needed to get a job and make some money as my savings had run out so on my return to London, I was sending out my CV like mad. It only took a month before I was back on a plane, headed to the Middle East again, planning to do it properly this time round.

On the flight to Damascus I tried to envision whether I would still be dancing there like I did in Egypt or speaking to the Goddess but I couldn't picture anything. I had a feeling Syria would be nothing like Egypt though. I had taken a short trip to Jordan and it had been a relatively normal experience – nobody bat an eyelid at me when I walked down the street so I knew that not every Arab country was like Egypt, which had been so intense and suffocating in comparison. Looking at pictures of Syria's capital on the Internet, it was everything I had been looking for. It had an almost medieval feel to it like a mixture of what I loved about England mingled with the mysterious Arabic influence. It ticked all the spiritual boxes too; conjuring up images and offering remnants of places from the Bible that are still standing today. For me it was a win-win destination to live. I would make money, work, get free accommodation, my bills paid, get away from memories of Ryan in London and to top it off, I would encounter the next stage of my spiritual journey and receive the answers that Egypt hadn't been able to provide. I felt these would not involve paganism, as this was a Muslim country I was moving to. It was supposedly patriarchal. The Goddess couldn't possibly live in Damascus.

My friends assumed I was crazy for heading back to the Middle East for such a long period of time. They couldn't understand why I, with my whole life ahead of me, would commit 'social suicide' by upping and leaving the city where it was all 'hip and happening,' where my friends went out partying at warehouses in East London and where I had unlimited access to amazing shops, cafes and could wear skirts above the knee without worrying about offending anyone. Why did I go to a country unheard of by my fellow countrymen and elicited responses such as that by my best friend, who met me at our local pub so I could tell her the news.

"Syria? Where's that?" Rumi had been at the white wine and it always went straight to her head. I could have sworn her voice increased in volume by at least a hundred decibels and that she morphed into a character from *Eastenders*, every time she drank it. “Where's that when it's at 'ome?" Not exactly the reaction I was expecting but one I got used to over the next two years.

“Rumi, it’s in the Middle East. Near to Turkey, Iraq, Lebanon…. You know those countries right?” I laughed and looked skywards in a display of feigned frustration.

“Ohhh right.” I could practically hear her mulling this news over in her mind. I waited.

“Ere, don't ya ‘ave to wear all black?”

“No, Rumi.”

She took another swig from her glass. I took two. *How many times could I look forward to having this ridiculous conversation* I thought. The answer, I came to discover, was every time I spoke to *anybody* in the UK.

“Guess ya can’t drink alcohol then.” She looked sadly into her massive glass of wine as though she were imagining never seeing a bottle of Pinot ever again.

“I’m moving to Syria. Not Saudi. You’re confusing Syria with Saudi aren’t you?”

“No I’m not.” She shouted. “I just can’t believe you’re leaving – for two years!” she finished off her glass and slammed it onto the table “and to a place nobody’s even heard of!” I couldn't argue with that. We both went quiet. Then her pretty, almond eyes lit up with recognition, her dead-straight, black hair, flicking back and forth with the excitable motion of her head.

"Ohhhh Syria! I know Syria! Ain’t that where Bin Laden's from?" After I had stopped laughing enough to talk, I reassured her that he wasn't and she became serious and asked if I was leaving because of everything that had been happening with Ryan. She knew that neither of us had really reached a resolution regarding the end of our relationship. We occasionally still saw each other in the short amount of time I had been back in London and we weren’t taking definitive action to cut contact. We were just drifting along, side-by-side, not wanting to pursue a relationship but not willing to let go completely. He thought it was a spiritual sign from the universe, telling us that we were meant to be forever but I just felt trapped. I supposed I was too afraid to be hurt by him again.

“I don't know.” I sighed.

Rumi and I had known each other since we were eleven but I shied away from letting my friends know when I was upset and I usually did a decent job of disguising it but that evening, I felt transparent in front of her. I hoped she couldn't see into my heart where the incident with the horrible Egyptian caretaker replayed itself again and again, where the hopes of a life with Ryan glinted and glimmered at me like diamonds, trying to entice me to pick them up, run my fingers over them and hold them to my throat. As much as I feared my friend stealing a peek into my heart, I suspected she couldn't. It was a closed door now. The sacred marriage ceremony and the caretaker made sure of that and I wasn't willing to open it ever again.

Chapter 16

The first three weeks of my arrival in Damascus involved a lot of signing papers, teaching, looking at houses and for vegetarian food to eat. The school put me up in a hotel while I sorted out accommodation.

"It's not as fun as it sounds!" I whined to Rumi over the phone. "I have to wash my clothes in the dry cleaner and eat out all the time. I swear I'm getting so fat right now. I can only eat pizza because these people are obsessed with meat!" Rumi's voice sounded like leaving the television on when you're home alone: safe and companionable.

"It sounds like a lot of stress but you will get through. Have you found a house yet?"

I explained that I had and that I was waiting to move in as the landlord was installing a new washing machine and having the place cleaned. And then the phone made a funny noise and cut out. Paranoid, I hung up and couldn't help but sneak a peak through the window onto the road far below: the *Mukhabarat* or *secret police*. I had heard a lot about them from my students already. They were always watching. Were they suspicious because I was making phone calls to the UK? Come to think of it, earlier that day I had rung my friend in the States. The Syrian government didn't like America very much. They didn't have McDonalds and had their own version of Coca Cola because of its perceived connection to Israel. They didn't like Israel very much either. My boss informed me on my first teaching day, not to refer to Israel but to say 'Palestine' instead. It was also a blocked search on *Google* and *Facebook* and *Youtube* were banned. That had taken me some getting used to.

I sprawled out on my king size bed, exhausted. I wondered if I should write a moaning email to my mum about my experience so far but remembered the secret police and thought I had better not. What if they had a device to read emails? What if they arrested me for not portraying Syria in a positive light? Instead, I checked my inbox and found that Ryan had written to me! I was stunned. I hadn't told him I moved to Damascus and we hadn't spoken for almost two weeks. We shared no mutual friends but that was just one of the many instances indicative of a spiritual connection between us. We were still so lost in each other that it wasn't easy to distinguish any part of myself from his influence on my life. Yet here he was as the last to know I had gone because I hadn't been able to bring myself to tell him. I knew if I had that he may have begged me to stay, or at the very least, his beautiful eyes would have begged me to and I wouldn't have been able to deal with the guilt. I kept thinking, *if Ryan hadn't cheated, I wouldn't have had to go on this journey. I would still be safe at home and things would be how they used to be.*

I cried as I typed the email informing him of my new home although I knew I would eventually have to pull myself together and get on with things. It was a new beginning for me now and I was determined to enjoy it, especially moving into my own place for the first time. *I am an adult now! I must try to forget about Ryan,* commonsense told me. For once, I listened.

A translator who worked for the school had taken me to look at flats and we had found a beautiful one in Taliani, an affluent area of Damascus, which means 'Italy'. It had two balconies with ornate metal decoration for railings, and it was so big it had two seven foot white doors that opened inwards with small windows above them. Radiators (unusual in Syria) were fitted in every room for the chilly winters and the floors were marble with green specks of color woven into the white design. I loved the enormously high ceilings and the windows that stretched from top to bottom. Windows lined the hallway from end to end, bordered by freshly painted pure white walls and bright green-leaved plants crawled along the ceiling. If you looked down, you could see into the first floor flat, which was in fact a typical Arabic house, complete with an open air living room with orange trees, blue, red and white tiling in oriental patterns as well as a fountain. It had been abandoned and was filled with broken glass and dust blown in from the desert, but I often spent time just observing the goings on down there, especially as a family of cats had decided to move in and I have a special place in my heart for felines.

Aside from the ugly Italian furniture in over the top gold and green, I felt like a princess in my stunning apartment and set about spending hundreds of pounds to do it up. I am a Virgo and love my home to look perfect and welcoming for guests. If that wasn't exciting enough, at the end of my road, there was a church inhabited by a few Irish and Italian nuns and monks, complete with Friar Tuck dress, and opposite my balcony at the front of my building were a mosque and the 'Italian hospital'. In this country, Christians and Muslims live side by side, an attribute that I noticed instantly and that which seemed to be a source of pride for the Syrian people. I learnt this very early on. I was never sure how tolerant they were towards other faiths but I did later meet a Buddhist family who felt pressured into pretending they were Muslim to the outside world whilst another Christian student confided in me that he was friends with a Syrian Jew; again unheard of. In fact I learnt a lot from my adult and young students in class, who often taught me inadvertently all I had to know to survive in the Damascus community. They were fascinated with me, having had little contact with the outside world, and although most were from the wealthiest three percent in the country, some of whom were actors and famous singers, as well as being related to senior politicians, they had never travelled outside Syria before. They would invite my colleagues and I to explore the city with them. They often led us down narrow lanes within the 'Old City' that wound around warrens of ancient houses, still inhabited by Damascene families, and lively bazaars that throbbed with life. Market sellers would thrust samples of their wares under our noses – fistfuls of nuts, sweets and brightly colored spices, urging us to have a taste. The air smelt of cumin and jasmine and the sound of coins jangling in pockets and Arabic radio playing a tinny sounding *Fairuz* followed us throughout the souq.

Piles of rugs, throws and cushion covers on tables lined the roads: silk dyed in a thousand combinations of shades of golds, reds, yellows, oranges and belly-dance outfits bordered with gold, glinted and caught our eye in the bright sunlight. There were the mysterious Iranian women dressed all in black, pushing roughly past us, headed for the ancient mosque. Men drank tea outside their shops on little stools, their turquoise and silver trays of shai glasses, waiting for guests to have a taste, hoping the power of the tealeaves would urge us to buy. My personal favorites were the artists who painted their pictures in the open air. Passers-by watch as the image of a whirling dervish comes to life from an easel, his spiral dance often portrayed as a pathway to unite with mankind and the entire universe. I bought a few paintings depicting a dervish dancing in the stars because I recognized myself in those pictures. I knew what it was like to try to dance reality away, as many of us do without realizing – getting drunk and going out with friends to a club when we feel upset counts too!

I found out that seven ancient doors surround the Old City and with names such as paradise gate and peace gate, I was enthralled with the spiritual implications these gateways may hold. The number seven is said to be magical and on researching the meaning of it I discovered that it is associated with not only death and rebirth but it is the number of the 'seeker' – the lifelong searcher of truth to be exact and is often connected with the search for the Holy Grail. Any other person might see no significance of ending up in a country I hardly knew anything about prior to my arrival with the fact that the city where I lived was surrounded by seven ancient doorways, but it was obvious to me that I had come to Damascus to be transformed. I couldn't believe I was now part of the oldest, continually inhabited city in the world. As my feet walked upon it, every step felt like gratitude to be witness to the beauty of such a mysteriously old land.

Chapter 17

Due to my experiences in Egypt and spending time in Turkey with family when I was young, I was pretty much prepared for the little every day things life in Syria might bring. However, I was not prepared for teaching in this country and it was a shock to the system. I had spent the previous four years teaching multilingual classes back in London which meant that there were a variety of cultures that made up one group of learners and that we could all retain our own identities. Now, I was the minority – an outsider in a class of Arabs and I had to adapt to their culture. In one lesson I instructed the students to prepare a short presentation on someone they admire.

"Are you ready?" I asked the most boisterous guy in the class. "Would you be able to give your talk now?"

"Yes, teacher." He said loudly so that everyone could hear. He motioned to the others to be quiet, putting on a big display in moving to the front of the room. I sat at the back, ready with my pen and paper in hand to note down some useful points he could work on to improve his presentation style.

"Ready! Go!" I beamed across at him, happy that he had been willing to present and didn't moan about it. He coughed and began,

"Teacher asked us to do a talk on someone we admire and the person I truly aspire to be like is Adolf Hitler." I felt my mouth drop open and words catch in my throat. As though he were telling us about how he enjoyed eating bananas, he continued, "Partly because he was a good leader and I want to be a leader someday, but mainly because he killed all the Jews."

I went to stand up to say something but stopping me from doing so was the rest of the class, nodding away as though they had heard this before. It was mundane to them; it was average, it was normal. The next four speakers all announced their hero to be Hitler too. When I asked my colleagues about it, pale-faced, they just nodded.

"Yup, that's pretty much what most of them say," they had responded. "Don't worry. You'll get used to it." The whole thing reminded me of something Ryan had said once – that history is *his story*. It can be altered and adapted to fulfill the agenda of anyone including governments.

I agreed with one thing that day and that was that I had to get used to the culture and society. It was so far, like nowhere I had ever stayed long enough to learn about. On my first morning, my manager warned me that there would be 'secret police' in most of my classes. I dubbed them the not-so-secret police because they always, without fail, wore eighties-style leather jackets like members of a bizarre middle-aged motorcycle gang, but instead of bikes they had crumbling yellow taxis. My colleagues and I could spot them from a mile off. My manager though, went on to say that if a teacher brought up 'inappropriate subject matter,' we could be arrested and deported and then he went on to give me examples of teachers that had happened to in the past.

Students had also been known to go missing if they said something that could be construed as being against the government. Suffice to say, I was sometimes on tenterhooks in my first couple of months, wondering if there was a policeman in my classroom spying on me. I felt intensely paranoid in the beginning. One lesson I decided to teach the conditional sentence, including a 'what would you do if you were…' conversation game. Students turned over a card and would discuss the answer to the question. It was all going well until a group noticed a 'what would you do if you were president?' question card. A man picked it up, laughing his head off and boomed out across the room, that he couldn't even imagine what that would be like because it would never come true. My eyes almost popped out of my head as I grabbed it from him, read it and crumpled it up quickly in the palm of my hand, trying to get rid of the damning evidence. I hid it in my pocket and then visited every group, slyly depositing each copy of the question up my sleeve.

“I almost had a heart attack!” I told my colleagues afterwards. “I thought the secret police would burst in and arrest me for putting revolutionary thoughts into my class’ minds!”

“Well it’s true.” They had said. “You need to check all your materials for that kind of thing before you give them out.” Needless to say, I never played that game in Syria again.

There were good and bad points about working in this new culture though, as I came to discover over time, and one of the best things was my students. A lot of them were decent, inspiring people who were curious about Western society and aspired to study there, but there were clashes between our ways of living that they couldn't get their heads around. For instance, the school I was working for followed British protocol and therefore, British law. By law they were required to have fire drills every once in a while. A normal thing for a Brit, but I learnt they were pretty alien to the average Arab. One day the alarm sounded and I marched my students outside. They looked baffled and flustered, not quite understanding what was happening. On returning to the class half an hour later, an Iraqi man looked at me and gesticulated wildly asking where the fire was in broken English.

“It was just practice. There was no fire. Don't worry.” I said soothingly, thinking he was afraid. He blinked about five times, pointed under the table and raised his eyebrows before saying,

“In Baghdad, I go university. When alarm ring, the bombs is falling but we get under table and continue writing. Now, there no fire and we must leave building! Why?”

The guys in the class slapped him on the back in a show of ‘you da man’. I laughed and had to tell him that the British like to be prepared but I felt slightly in awe of this person who would put his education before life itself.

I also didn't understand how these people were going to study in the West if they didn't like public displays of affection. The morality police were called because a couple was seen kissing on the school roof terrace.

Yes. There is such a thing as the morality police.

They were called to ‘investigate’ and threatened the school with closure. Two burly men showed up in their eighties leather jackets. Heavily sun tanned hands lit cigarettes in front of a no smoking sign.

“Where are they?” Barked one at the center manager in Arabic.

“What are you teaching here? Grammar or Immorality?” chided the other in accusatory tones.

The Welsh manager looked as though he was apologizing profusely in his admirable grasp of Arabic. His face and neck was breaking out in a crimson rash and I couldn't blame him for feeling panicked. Those policemen had the authority to be brutal and from what I understood, basically ran Damascus. Luckily, he seemed to be winning them over. I observed their faces lighten up instantly with the appearance of more cigarettes and fresh coffee brought over by the boy who worked for the school's café. The local teacher, who had translated for me and our other colleagues as we watched from the other side of the room, put her hand over her mouth to disguise her amusement.

"They were acting like it was a murder mystery," she whispered through bursts of stifled laughter.

The idea that a secret policeman could walk around as a representation of 'morality' was laughable to me. These are the same men who supposedly torture people for information and could lock you up for something as simple as not having the president's face beaming out from your car window. In the beginning, I was incredibly nervous in this country where everything was so different and so unpredictable and where you could get in trouble with the authorities at the drop of a hat.

However, my colleagues and I generally felt that Syrians were a very hospitable people even if there were a lot of rules to abide by. I got to know a lot of the locals very well, including some who were working at the school as teachers and in the office. They seemed to be interested in me and were constantly speculating about my origins. This was something I was accustomed to having grown up in London on a council estate in Hackney, in the middle of the nineties. I felt I fit in well with the community though as it was one of the most multi-cultural parts of London, with large Caribbean, Irish, African, Asian and Turkish communities and being half Turkish on my father's side, I found that there was always somewhere I belonged. When we were younger, my friends often remarked that people were staring at me in the street because they were trying to figure out where I came from. Curly, brown hair hung to the middle of my back and in summer I tanned easily. Hazel eyes reveal my mother's English side as well as my pale skin in the winter. I had always been regarded as tall and thin, and as my Jamaican best friend would say,

"Your lips are bigger than mine gal!" Sometimes we had 'whose lips are the biggest' competitions and braided my hair in cane rows and that was fun, however, this doubt regarding my origins in Damascus suggested an underlying hostility. Most Syrians decided I was 'Arab pretending to be British', whilst the Armenian Syrians I befriended, concluded that I pretended to not understand Turkish and all of my students determined that I was 'Syrian posing as Brit'. The reason? I did not have blonde hair and blue eyes and that was how British people were 'supposed to look'. The frustration I felt at times was off the scales, mainly due to being judged as less capable as an English teacher because of my appearance. I was not the only one to suffer. A fellow teacher with Indian origins, but born and raised in England, elicited complaints to the manager stating that her 'Indian accent was incomprehensible'. Her English accent was more upper class than all of the office put together!

"Syrians see themselves as lower than a white person," whispered one of our more out-spoken colleagues one evening. "Haven't you noticed that they are always making jokes at their own expense?" Five of us – Canadians and Brits were at our favorite hangout: the Indian restaurant round the corner in *Shaalan.* We all nodded in unison at his words – it really did seem that way. Their lack of faith in myself and other colleagues as a teacher, based solely on our hair color, served only to suggest that they found themselves, unable to teach effectively. Students did often comment on how their English language classes at school had been terrible as they were only ever allowed to copy from the board and memorize grammar rules. I take a more learner-centered approach, which encourages students to be the focus of the lesson rather than the teacher, and yet my classes hated it! They weren't used to taking responsibility for their learning and craved a teacher who constantly told them what to do. They didn't like group work because they didn't want to learn from each other and 'pick up each others' mistakes' and they wanted me to correct all of their spoken errors.

With some classes I did give in to their demands as paying customers, standing at the front of the class as 'the fountain of all knowledge' and completely ignoring the contributions these students could make to their own learning because that was what made them happy. With others I tried to experiment. Funnily enough I could see the parallels clearly between the type of learning experience they expected and the dictatorship the country was under; people sitting quietly at their desks, unquestioning while the authority figure who 'knows what's best for them,' tells them what to do.

"Did you know that no foreigners are allowed into a state school?" outspoken colleague continued. "Makes you wonder what they're hiding." He didn't have to wonder that much though. He was living in Syria with his wife and two children.

"Don't your kids tell you?" I asked curiously and I was met with a smug grin. He was about to impart some wisdom. He always seemed to know so much about what was *really* going on in Syria and yet he should have been on the outside like the rest of us and treated only with suspicion. There were rumors going around that he was some sort of spy.

"The kids – as soon as they enter the school system – spend hours outside chanting allegiance to the president. As if they have any other choice!" He laughed loudly at his own joke and half chewed particles of food sprayed out of his mouth. He was fluent in Arabic and recited what the children are trained to say for us in English.

"I would give my right arm for the president. Chop off my legs for the president. I will give my life for him. I will die for him." He looked at us, his blue eyes searching for a reaction. "My four year old is forced to shout this come rain or shine in the playground for hours everyday."

It was true. There was a school opposite my kitchen and I saw the kids out there and heard their robotic chants drift up and into my open windows. Now I knew what they were saying. We all shook our heads in horror and tutted. The regime took them when they were young.

There was a reason why my father had to flee Turkey as a university student, I thought as I walked home that night. University is the only opportunity many people around the world have to start critically analyzing things for themselves. Students are the biggest threat to a country's government: young - still young enough to fear nothing until it is upon them, motivated, riled up by inspired literature, egged on by great figures in history, university students often have access to information far beyond the reach of the average shop owner or farmer in the middle East. So when the young people of a country are in the education system, a government uses that time to their advantage. They bend and mold those minds to fit their agenda but it doesn't always work. For instance, a talented student of mine invited me out for lunch. Mohamad was a medical student at Damascus University. Not the tallest of guys, his jet-black hair and smiley demeanor ensured that he was always the center of attention and could light up the dullest of rooms. He loved chatting about anything and everything and he had big dreams. He was also, the only Syrian person within my initial two year stay in Damascus, who one day whispered to me in a secluded side street in Qassar, a Christian quarter of the city, that he wanted the regime to fall. He actually laughed as he recalled the last election prior to 2009 in which Assad had claimed to win over the general population with a 99.99 percent of the vote.

"99.99 percent!" He exclaimed and it came out half snort and half indignation and his outburst may as well have been a gunshot. I could have sworn people were looking, listening, ready to identify us to the secret police. "Do they think we are stupid?" I nervously looked around and gave a fake smile, wishing he would be quiet. And then I realized how a government was able to keep people from questioning. Pure fear. *If my family had been in Syria with me*, I thought, *I would have walked away from him right then and there, for the danger he was putting me in.*

Even worse was being affiliated with a British organization as a Syrian national. A close friend and colleague of mine told of getting the 'knock on the door' whereby you were escorted to a secret location to be interviewed by the police.

"What did they ask you?" I whispered, eyes like saucers. She looked past me, remembering.

"My mum was panicking."

"Oh no, your poor mum!" She started to stir some tea in a pot on the ornate, over the top and completely characteristic Arabic coffee table in front of her: a heavy marble slab on top of marble legs that curled outward. Some moments passed and I later wondered if the pause was her contemplating what to say and what to leave out.

"They asked me if I loved my country. They knew my parents are not originally Syrian. They asked if I would fight for my country and if I would protect it." She paused again and I knew what she was going to say. "They asked me to spy on the school."

I wondered how a country could be built on paranoia. The government was paranoid about their people, the people were paranoid about the government, and the government was paranoid about anyone who was not Syrian. We saw the American tourists wandering about the old city and thought they were brave for being there in 2009. Their naiveté started off as endearing but soon became exasperating as they marveled at the stunning mosques in bright whites and turquoise hues and remarked on their 'relaxing' songs of prayer. Little did they know that the Imam was actually calling out 'death to America' in Arabic. After providing a home for thousands upon thousands of people displaced in the war on Iraq, still ongoing at the time, it was inevitable that tensions would be running high.

On the other hand, it is important to note that this was not a sentiment shared by the average Syrian person. After work, I would go along with colleagues and students from all over the world, to roof top parties in the old city and *Straight Street* - the same street visited by Saint Paul as mentioned in the Bible but ironically now lined with clubs and bars. Actually, Damascus was where I drunk the most alcohol I have ever consumed in my entire life and had the most fun with my British and Syrian friends. The Americans who were studying Arabic at the university were a lot of fun too but I was bemused one evening at another rooftop party, on meeting a girl from Illinois, who was wearing a T-shirt with a picture of George Bush in the middle of a 'forbidden' symbol, like a No Smoking sign. And I found myself whispering to my friend,

“Wow. Guess she must be paranoid.”

Chapter 18

I made a friend waiting in line for an AIDS test. No, I had not *gone wild* in Damascus. I was merely applying for residency and this was part of it. I approached her. She was huddled in a corner looking terrified. I summed her up as being a nutcase drama queen but I thought I had better introduce myself to be polite. We were the only foreigners in the waiting room after all. She shook my hand and I wiped it against my clothes when she wasn't looking. It felt cold and clammy which made me laugh inwardly. What was the big deal? It's just a standard medical test. Then she said her name was Bibi and whispered,

"I swear those needles are dirty. Look at all those vials of blood. How will they know which one is mine? What if they mix them up? And look in that corner over there. Dust! Look at that crisp wrapper. Filth! This is a dirty hospital!" and I, fine up until then, totally freaked out too. "One guy at work said this very place diagnosed him with..." and she hesitated before finishing with a dramatically mouthed, "AIDS! … But he didn't have it really. He had to go back to England and everything!"

That sent me over the edge and by the time the nurse came in to get us, we had worked ourselves into a frenzy, both cowering in the corner and were gibbering wrecks. We bonded over the experience though and managed to laugh about it when we got the all clear a few weeks later. We had both moved to Damascus at roughly the same time and learnt about living there together.

"Ya' know," I said to her as we walked down *Abu Rumaneh* on a lovely spring day. We were going to meet my student who had offered to take us up to *Qassoon mountain* for dinner. "I never expected Syria to be so open-minded regarding homosexuality." Bibi looked at me, one eyebrow raised.

"What do you mean?"

"Well," I said, "look at those two guys over there holding hands and those two! Look! Did you see that? They just kissed on the cheek! All in the cold light of day!" I didn't get why my friend was now laughing and pointing at me. "Okay Bibi, what? They're not gay?" She took forever to stop laughing.

"That's what men do here Tina you nutter! They aren't gay! They are just friends."

"Alright … well they are acting gay! How was I supposed to know?" I retorted, giggling a bit too.

"You said it like you wanted to give Syria a Nobel peace prize for being open-minded! Actually being gay is illegal here!" Bibi made fun of me some more and I was glad I had said it to her and nobody else. They would probably have thought I was really dumb. Just then a car horn cut through our laughter and my student was in front of us, reaching over to the passenger seat door to open it for me. We both piled in and Bibi embarrassed me by explaining to my student how I had thought Syria was a gay haven as he drove.

"Trust me," he said laughing. "There are no gays here." I didn't believe it but smiled at him anyway, shaking my head.

Bibi and I marveled at the views as we climbed the roads leading up to a bunch of restaurants that lined the mountain's edge. The sun was setting which made it all the more magical.

"I love twilight," I remarked as we got out of the car and headed toward a restaurant. We sat outside and breathed in the fresh air, ordering cocktails and small dishes of humous, taboulleh, muhamra and lots of my favorite spinach pastries. I felt so glad to be there and so... *free.* Nobody made any comments or stared at us any longer than what was necessary for them to discern that we were foreigners. The waiters were polite; the food was great and the atmosphere peaceful. It was the first time I had felt stable in ages; I had money coming in regularly, my inviting house was always waiting for me and work was pretty much what I was used to.

We were listening wide eyed to my student tell us about when he got his thirteen year old girlfriend pregnant at age fourteen and had to go into hiding for a year because her father wanted to kill him when we realized it was eleven at night.

"It's so late! I have to be up at seven tomorrow – so early for me!" said my student. Syrian people did not like getting up in the morning – they considered eight, early.

"You should try getting up at six like I used to back in London," Bibi joked. He made a face and we hobbled back to the car, a little tipsy.

"I'm still in shock!" I exclaimed. "Teen pregnancy happens in the Middle East too?"

"I love her even now." He said, a far away look in his eyes.

"But that was ten years ago!" Bibi responded and in her abrupt way said "you have to get over it now. Every Syrian man I meet seems to have this story about the *one who got away*. Like a girl they got with who they knew their family wouldn't approve of but they stay with her anyway and then she gets engaged and married, leaving him broken hearted."

"Oh my gosh! That's so true!" I laughed. "My male students always have this story of a girl they were forced to break up with because she is a different religion or social class!"

The engine started up, my student muttered something about Syrian guys not being able to help it if they are romantic and we began the slow descent down the mountain on winding roads. About two minutes in, Bibi pointed out a car parked up on the corner.

"Aww that's adorable. They pimped out their car with little curtains on the windows! How cute!" I was just about to join in and comment on how quaint that was when my student burst out into laughter.

"Er hm… ladies… I think I should inform you that those curtains have another purpose. Look." He continued going down the road and showed us at least five other cars that had parked and had curtains on the window. All the curtains were drawn.

"This mountain is a great place for food… but also… sex!" Our mouths fell to the floor. "In Syria a man and woman can only rent a hotel room if they are married, so they come here instead."

"No. Way." Mouthed Bibi. We could only stare out of the window at amazement at the many, many cars lined up, curtains drawn.

"That one's rocking!" I shouted. "It's rocking!" Bibi plastered her hands and face to the window to get a better look. My student stopped so we could see: weirdest porno ever.

"They are probably having sex in her ass," added my student, as if we weren't stunned enough by the revelations of the night so far. He took advantage of our inability to speak,

"So he doesn't break her virginity and she can marry as a lovely clean virgin."

"That's… that's… so fucking sexist! Why does she have to be a virgin? Does he have to be one too?" Bibi asked in indignation, her voice rising in anger.

"Nope! Of course not! We are encouraged to sleep with Russian prostitutes so we don't defile our virginal women!" He was in hysterics whilst Bibi and I maintained disgusted looks on our faces for the rest of the way home. Nothing he did could make us smile.

"I'm never getting with a Syrian guy if that's how they are," I said, crossing my arms. "Never! I would rather be a TEFL victim!" TEFL (teaching English to foreign language speakers) victims, as they are affectionately known in the English teaching world are those people, typically over forty who live all over and are unable to settle down with anyone because they have spent their entire lives running from something or other. Either that or they like their jobs so much they have sacrificed what is deemed a 'normal' life. To be a female TEFL victim is worse than being a male TEFL victim because people just assume you have serious issues or are a lesbian. I often looked at the TEFL victims in the staff room and prayed I wouldn't end up like them. I didn't want to be alone forever, forced from one country to the next, having to get used to a new culture all over again. But I still had another year and a half to go before I could get back to England. I would be twenty-nine and then it would probably take a year to find a boyfriend, date him for two years, get engaged for another two, get married and have a baby – another year.

"I will be almost in my late thirties by the time I get to have kids!" I said to Bibi over some wine one night, panic tingeing my voice. "What if my biological clock like… runs out of batteries or something? What if I can't have kids Bibi because I stayed in Syria too long?"

"Syrian guys are hot, Tina. Just go on a few dates, see what they're like. They can't all be sexist pigs!" She replied loudly into my ear to be heard over a squealing Arabic song. She pointed out some cute guys in the corner of the bar and sniggered about how short they were compared to me. I laughed her suggestion off but inside, I was seriously considering it.

Chapter 19

The truth was that I longed to be seen as part of Damascus society. I can't pinpoint exactly what triggered it but it crossed my mind that maybe this was a new development in the search for myself. After all, I had been in Syria for five months now and had barely had a spare moment to consider anything even remotely spiritual – unless 'spiritual' was the new word for 'to party' that is.

At first my soul needed to belong on a global level like observing how the women looked and behaved and emulating them in some ways. Then I wanted to speak like they did and share the same jokes as a Syrian would. I found myself becoming interested in their arts and culture, listening carefully to opinions, and learning how society worked. And this longing lay beneath the surface of my consciousness and the only way I knew it existed was when I looked out from my balcony and saw couples holding hands on the yellow street below, and good friends gossiping in cafes, heavily painted lips hidden by Argile pipes as they laughed and shared Syrian secrets.

Somehow this desire to be part of Damascus was only further impounded by the subtle rejection I received daily. There were some disapproving looks by older women and the Arabic words that sounded like *sex* as I walked down a busy road. They made me feel dirty underneath my skin. But like anything dirty, I figured anything could come clean again. Although I had never articulated it in my own thoughts, I felt like soiled goods. After all, being part of Syrian society involved only one thing: marriage and children. In this country, it is essential that a woman is a virgin on her wedding night, be you Christian or Muslim. At now twenty-eight years old, almost half a year into my stay in Syria, I was… well… anything but. My age also ensured that I wasn't seen as appropriate marriage material. Twenty-five was generally the cut-off point. If the Oxford English dictionary allowed an untraveled, uneducated Arab man or woman to write a definition for the term *'Western woman'*, I got the impression it would read something like;

'Western woman'

Ready for sex at any moment. Chances of sex increase with this woman when you stare at her for long periods of time, follow her down the street and mumble. Chances increase further if you whisper, 'you me, fucky fuck?'

Example sentence: "That Western woman (n) will agree to relieve my horniness despite her never having met me in her life".

Example sentence 2: "She's Western (adj.) so she must want sex. With me. Now. Despite her never having met me in her life".

Synonyms: Porn Star, Prostitute, Horny.

I, somehow, formed the opinion that I could discard this image. Like, tear it out of their fucked up version of a dictionary that judges people by their hair, their eyes and their nationality and throw it up in the air, screaming "in your face motherfuckaaaa" kinda discard. So one night I decided to fall in love and get married. As though it were *that* easy. As though I could go to *Tescos* and put an Arab in my trolley, ready to go in his tux. Now, I know what you're thinking. Really I do. I'd done lost my mind. But the truth was that while I had no family in Damascus, I had friends. I wanted to soften their judgmental eyes when I mentioned my ex whom I had not been married to; didn't want them to have to tell me that, in Syria, things are different. I also wanted to have more respect when I walked down the street.

When I had lived in Egypt, men would grab at me and thrust cash in my face, hoping I was a prostitute. Syrian men were a lot more, subtle in their assumptions about me, but I knew they were there. If I so much as held the wrong man's gaze for a split second when I was out shopping, I would find him skulking behind clothes racks and grocery store shelves, spying on me, hours later in the hopes that glance had been a sexy invite. Although some people thought I *looked* Arab, the average Syrian knew I wasn't. But if I could become Syrian, maybe I could lay claim to everything that had ignited my fascination with the Arabs in the beginning. I could claim their beautiful history and a little part of the wisdom of an Arab woman could flow through my veins.

The divine feminine that encapsulates an Arab woman seemed to be expressed through her humility, her humbleness, her eyes. The elegance of a long skirt and long lashes that curl at the ends and kohl eyes cast downward, lips curled upwards in a sly smile. She is so aware of her femininity that she can cast it forth in ways I had never considered before. I wanted that and so I watched high society Syrian women closely, (mainly because they were the people whom I had close contact with through work) in case I might want to become more like them and marry a Syrian man. I learnt the following that I jotted down in my notebook so I wouldn't forget:

1. Avoid the sun at all times. The pale, ghostly look is in.
2. Visit the hairdresser every week and ask for the biggest, most poof-iest hairstyle you can.
3. If you can afford it, go to Beirut for the latest plastic surgery.
4. Wear a full set of makeup even if you are only going to the local

supermarket.

5. Matching red knee high boots and red coats are acceptable.

6. All clothes must have words written on them in extremely poor English. Props to those wearing sentences that don't make sense.

7. Wear high heels at all times, even in caves.

8. Unless a man is a doctor or dentist, he is not fit for the purpose of marriage.

I also tried to hang out with more of my female students so that I had the chance to learn more. I was an eager student. For instance, one girl in my class invited me for lunch with her and her mother and younger teenage brother. I had never been to visit her family before and her mother was very welcoming and kind, making vegetarian food especially for me. Accidently I complimented a wooden plaque on the wall with the Prophet Mohammad's name (PBUH) weaved into the shape of a five-pointed star and she was in the process of trying to stuff it into my bag. I say that my accolade was accidental because in Syria, it is culturally expected that if one is complimented on something, that item must immediately be turned over to its admirer. I had already accumulated several scarves, necklaces and rings that I didn't even like, all because I had wanted to make their owners feel pretty. What was considered a positive trait in the UK had become a burden in the Middle East!

"Please, please it is yours."

"Oh, oh! I can't take it. It looks so nice on the wall over there."

"Welcome." She shoves it into my bag anyway and that's that. It would now be considered rude for me not to take it. "You like sweet?" She shouted as she made her way into the kitchen. My student budged past her mother's large frame in their narrow hallway, with a tray full of syrup-laden parcels of deliciousness. I chose my favorite desert of *kunefe* and we began eating. Her mother entered the room again with tea and as she poured, she began to tell me about the girl downstairs whom her son would soon become engaged to. She was beaming with pride and her young son had the biggest smile on his face.

"She is the most beautiful girl in our area. Everybody thinks she is amazing."

I just smiled back, chewing my last bit of the cheesy-honey desert. I didn't understand the obsession with beauty in this country. Was there nothing else to say about this girl?

"Go get her Riza," she said to him in Arabic, ushering him out of the room.

Awkward. She would think I had asked to look at her like a donkey for sale in the market.

As he disappeared from view, the rather plump, excitable woman, whose English wasn't at all bad, mouthed, gesturing to her arms and face, “Her skin so, so white. So beautiful.”

I sit back into cushions, crease my forehead contemplatively and from all the hype start wondering what this girl would look like. The woman uses more positive adjectives and my student looks at me as if to say, *get ready for the Syrian Angelina Jolie*. Eyes fixed on the door; a head finally pops around it. The palest, sickest looking girl I had ever seen. Never mind getting engaged, this girl needed to be consuming some red meat and fast. Yes her skin was white, but her face was slightly deformed at the jaw line, which confirmed that Syrians would overlook features that could be undesirable, in favor of pale skin.

From that day forth, I walked in the shade to achieve the desirable Syrian pale look. I figured I might be able to play on the sacredness of a beautiful woman here to achieve my goal of marriage. But damnit! I already seemed to be in perma-tan phase because Syria never saw a cloudy sky between March and September every year! On my way home in the taxi, listening to the driver playing *Fares Karem* – a fitting tune about a man who misses his home country - I considered the paradox that people want to ‘fit in’ to their surroundings and yet, beauty is always considered to be the exact opposite to how the people of that society actually look. We all want what we can't have. We all think perfection is elsewhere I realized and strive to achieve it 'tomorrow'. I couldn't help but wonder if everything would be different if we all just decided to live for today.

In fact, Syrian women are a lot more concerned about their future and it meant I had to be as well, if I were to be more like them. "Who am I going to marry?" would be the most popular question, considering marriage was the very fabric of the Syrian community. Sara – my Syrian colleague at work - used to take that very question to the local city wise woman or 'psychic', over and over and over again. We grew close because of our shared interest in spirituality whereas Bibi didn't believe in any of that *mumbo jumbo* as she called it.

Sara was fascinated with this woman and so one evening, she asked me to come along. We set off in one of the city's many yellow taxis, to see her.

"What are you going to ask her?" Sara squealed. I thought she was going to faint with the anticipation.

"I don't know, but I know what you will."

"You don't! No way! Go on then, guess! You can't guess! Eeee!" she bounced up and down in her seat, her voice so high pitched in excitement I was sure only dolphins could hear her.

"If you and Larry will marry right?" I asked, monotone, trying to conceal my smile.

"You got meeee."

I personally knew Sara had been to see this woman about fifteen times and each time had asked her the same question. I considered asking the psychic woman whom I would marry but I hadn't met anyone I liked, so I figured that would be pointless. Sara's squeals were still ringing in the deep, dark depths of my ear canal, when the taxi came to a halt. We were somewhere in the suburbs. In fact we appeared to be surrounded by some fields. I had rarely ventured that far out of Damascus in a taxi before. It was pitch black and there were huge puddles in the dilapidated roads leading up to her property. Sara paid the driver and we walked up to the door to knock but a small boy opened it before we could. There was some commotion as the boy ran inside to inform his mother she had more customers. Sara pointed to a brand new car parked in front of the building and said that it belonged to the woman. I raised my eyebrows. This woman must be making some serious dough!

The boy, who had opened the door, led us to a room off of the central living area which was open air as most typical Arabic houses were throughout the city. I was stunned by the size of the place and could tell that they had tried to keep it modest. Oddly enough, Sara mentioned that this woman was Muslim. I had always been told it was *Haram* or *forbidden* to ask about the future within Islam but she obviously wasn't lacking customers.

As we were led to a sofa and brought tea and cakes, Sara started speaking to a teenage girl who I assumed was the woman's daughter. I couldn't understand them so I looked around the room. My palms were sweating. *What on Earth was I going to witness?* I thought as images of people on the Egypt tour came back to me, some channeling past life memories, others just rolling around on the floor screaming. I should probably have taken a break from all this psychic stuff but as usual my curiosity overwhelmed me. I must surely have lived before as a cat. *Oh goodness those people from the Egypt trip have rubbed off on me.* I smiled to myself, remembering.

On the walls there were framed pieces of calligraphy. Probably verses from the Qu'ran. There were a lot of rugs strewn about haphazardly and many Holy books in glass cabinets. It smelled of incense and old pages and it felt like prayer. I knew it was a prayer room because I felt light headed and floaty. As though a whooshing were flowing through my toes and out of my head. I was enjoying the sensation when the woman entered the room. She was extremely pretty through her modest dress: a little chubby but from the looks of the kids running about, she had probably been pregnant ten times. Her hair looked gorgeous with blonde highlights running through it and her skin was a soft caramel color. She looked only about thirty-eight. Her smile, unlike a lot of pretty Syrian girls I had met, was welcoming and genuine.

After greetings, Sara – a Catholic - began asking the usual questions about the guy she was seeing and marriage. This was a typical scene in Syria so absent in the rest of the Middle East: people of different faiths, respecting the beliefs of each other. The woman got comfy in her chair and put her headscarf over her head. I looked on. Suddenly she raised her hands up above her and her eyes gazed at them. She was holding Islamic prayer beads. She started to rock her body back and forth and move the beads around, one by one, arms, still up in the air. And then she giggled. Her face creased in joy and her eyes were tightly closed as she started answering the questions in Arabic in a child's voice. It was as though the spirit of a little girl had entered her body. She couldn't keep still. I must have looked like a deer in the fog lights. I didn't know if I should listen to Sara translating or if I should grab some of the frankincense and wave it in front of her face shouting "the power of Christ compels you." I had never witnessed anything like it before. I reluctantly decided upon the former, but way too soon, it was my turn. Sara looked ecstatic as she asked me what my question would be. Obviously she had got what she wanted to hear.

"Hmmm, I would really like to know about Hannah." Hannah was a spiritual teacher back in the UK who I had previously worked with. She was a good friend but was going through some tough times. Sara translated the request and there was a moment of silence as she looked back at me curiously. I thought I had imagined it as the woman proceeded to become the little girl again and tell me things that I later decided could be true for anyone. However, I hadn't. After a short discussion whereby I faked belief in the so-called psychic predictions in the taxi on the way home, Sara suddenly burst out laughing.

"She thought you were a lesbian!" I looked at her in indignation, annoyed that they had been laughing at me in a language I couldn't understand.

"What the fuck? I knew I shouldn't have worn this blazer with shoulder pads!"

I started to take off the offending jacket.

"No silly!" Sara was laughing too much to explain quick enough and now I was wearing a skimpy (by Syrian standards) tee shirt in a taxi with a strange driver in a weird area of Damascus I didn't know.

"She wondered if you were gay because you asked about a woman! You are the first girl in five years not to ask who you were going to marry!"

It was humiliating to be twenty-eight and single in the Middle East and I was getting sick of it however, the best thing I took away from this experience was the realization that there was a feminine energy floating through Syria. Visions of women huddled together in that house, praying for insight into their future husbands seemed so Goddess – like. I was ready to explore the magic that lay hidden in this ancient land.

Chapter 20

Every time I got out my deck of tarot cards I was reminded of Ryan's face that day at my dance workshop and his disapproval at my love of the divine feminine. The thing is, my love for her did not result in my intuitive side rather my intuitive side led me to her. Loving the Goddess gave me a point of reference regarding where my psychic experiences originate from and made me appreciate my womanhood. But after all I had experienced in the Middle East so far I wasn't completely sure if the Goddess was welcome there in Syria. I wondered if I should stuff her deep down inside me along with Primal woman. The students at the school wouldn't hear of it.

"Teacher! Please bring your cards tomorrow!" They had begged, and I had reluctantly agreed. Now there I was, sixteen students gathered around my desk and my cards spread out in front of me.

"I had a dream that I was shopping for rings." Said one woman, face eager, eyes searching me for what it meant.

"Oh that definitely means there's a man waiting in the sidelines. You don't know him yet but he is planning to ask you to marry him."

The class gasped and started chirping away in Arabic. I didn't understand what they were saying but it didn't matter. I knew I would be proved right very soon. A young, hyper lady – a bit of a chatterbox – made sure she had her turn. A pretty girl with dark brown hair who played the flute in an orchestra sat in the seat opposite me and laid her hands over the cards. I told her to pick them up and shuffle them and she did. I had a sense she would be easy to read.

"Divide them into three piles," I whispered, smiling, trying to sound mysterious for everybody's entertainment. The class laughed and I chose the middle pile and overturned them to reveal their colorful pictures. *Uh oh*, I thought. *The Tower*. I had gotten that card before I discovered that Ryan had cheated on me. As I put them into position I shook my head. This wasn't going to be good.

"I'm sorry but your boyfriend is cheating on you." I am unapologetically blunt as a reader. I expected her to react but I didn't expect her to laugh. She laughed until she cried.

"What? My boyfriend? That's hilarious! He would never, ever do that! He doesn't have the guts!" She laughed some more and we all just shrugged our shoulders and got on with the rest of the readings.

I did not see that girl again in my classes until a couple of months later when I bumped into her in the street. My beloved gold bangles – a gift from my mother – dug into me as she grabbed me by the wrist and pulled me into the nearest café saying she had to tell me something and that she needed another reading.

"Tina! It came true! On the very same day!" I just looked at her, not understanding. "The reading was true! He was cheating on me." I said I was sorry and she proceeded to tell me what happened. "The same day you did my tarot, I got on the bus to go home from school and as I looked out of the window, about ten minutes into my journey, I saw him walking down the street – my boyfriend holding hands with another girl!" My mouth fell open as she relayed this to me.

"What did you do?" I asked, fascinated.

"Well I jumped out of the bus and approached him and he admitted everything. Well he couldn't deny it could he? She was right there! They were actually in a real relationship despite me having been with him for the past five years!"

"Oh my God," was all I could say as I shook my head in dismay.

"Now, he is in a relationship with her!"

After that incident, word spread that I could read futures. I wasn't that into tarot though and preferred other methods but it didn't stop people from knocking on my door requesting advice on one thing or another.

Sometimes I would sew friends and students mojo bags which are small pouches in relevant colors – for example pink for love and fill them with herbs and crystals to help a wish come true. A few people also asked me to decode their dreams as the woman I had interpreted the ring - shopping dream for, was engaged two weeks later but I had to be very discreet about it. Tarot decks were illegal in Syria from what I understood, plus Sara told me that the psychic woman we had gone to see was paid a visit by the secret police who wanted to know if she had psychic access to any government knowledge. She had to reassure them that she was only interested in giving readings to people based on who they would marry and nothing else. This scared me because I didn't want the secret police knocking on my door.

A part of me felt uneasy, communicating with that side of myself again but I understood it was due to me feeling awkward in my own skin as a woman - a result of the experiences I had undergone in the Middle East thus far. I was having occasional nightmares about the caretaker and I had a couple of dodgy experiences with men on the streets of Damascus that required police intervention but it was nothing that scared me away – the police were very effective in their handling of the two cases. Thc experiences merely left me aware that as a Western woman, I was viewed in a way that I didn't appreciate by a tiny minority of men who didn't know how to behave in civilized society.

One of my favorite classes begged me for a reading one morning out of the blue. Undeterred by the fact that I didn't have my cards with me, I figured I would try something else. I was a witch wasn't I? We make do with whatever we have to hand! I instructed the guys to go get me water in a dark colored bowl from the café downstairs. I was going to try my hand at scrying – the act of seeing the past, present or future in liquid. They gathered around it excitedly, all the while keeping an ear out for foot falls on the steps. If my bosses caught me doing this during class time there would be big trouble!

Wala was a pretty girl and totally free-spirited. She never really came across as a studious young lady and it was obvious she had come to the British school to find a husband! I asked if she would go first and she reluctantly nodded, a fearful little smile on her face.

"Sit opposite and look down into the water." She did as instructed and I gave a little wave. "Do you see my reflection in there as well as yours?" She nodded again. "That's why the container needs to be dark." The students' eyes widened and I asked Wala to focus on the watery mirror. We both gazed down and I must say that I did not expect this to work at all. I was just wondering if I should make something up for a laugh when all of a sudden a picture flashed into my mind from nowhere. Actually I can't say the picture was in my head, rather it seemed to have been a vision I had seen with my eyes. It was so clear. Wala was lying on a surgery table in hospital and there were three doctors around her, operating on her stomach. I relayed this to her and almost had a heart attack,

"B.b.but I… haven't told anyone about that! Not even my best friends!" She cried, tears dropping into the dark water. "I am having a stomach operation this Saturday!"

We all just stared at each other, mouths agape. I was as shocked as they were. Instead of the fearful looks I had become accustomed to whenever I had 'visions' back in London, they erupted into squeals of "Do mine! Do mine!" and I spent another hour scrying for them.

I was ecstatic that I had been able to scry and communicate so effectively with one of the elements. Tarot was good but scrying was a way to link with nature and Mother Earth herself. I intuited the Goddess by my side there in that foreign land and I began to see her everywhere I looked. I was of the opinion that she would get me into trouble though as I knew that I would start to connect with my emotions again and pick up vibes from the people around me. It's sort of like becoming water… going with the flow, tears come easier, I can sense a full moon and when the rain is about to fall and the stars remind me of something. *But it is okay*, I told myself. *The Goddess is calling right now. Answer.*

Chapter 21

Proof that I had found the Goddess in Syria lay in my frequent visits to Saydnaya with Sara, which is a Christian city in the outskirts of Damascus. Although I say the city is Christian, I mean its historical origins lie in Christianity and can be traced back well over a thousand years. Muslims do live there. I have a dear friend who is from the first Islamic family to make Saydnaya their home. I absolutely loved it. Everything was a sandy yellow when you were in the mountains and down below, there were winding, cobbled streets and old grey town houses. The only color was made up of pictures of Jesus and the Virgin Mary. Golds, reds and blues hung in shop windows and cars. Green fields spread out for miles. Green was not a shade one saw often in the capital. I decided I would never take the greenness of London for granted again after I witnessed first hand how human beings need to be close to nature but don't even realize it. The highways around Damascus were full of picnicking families sitting on the grass embankments, their bodies desperate to feel that natural connection to the Goddess we all have. I would stare at them with a smug, knowing smile on my face. Arab men were appreciating the divine feminine!

Sara would pack a bag with pink and white candles and dried rose petals and we would write wishes on paper we could burn and release to the winds. We prayed together for the one thing we all want deep down. Love. And the one thing I still thought would redeem me – marriage. I surmised that if I were married to a Syrian man, I would be able to show society that I was desirable and that I was worthy – that he had married me because I was *good.*

One day, Sara wanted to leave a little offering of gold in the ancient Orthodox Catholic church on top of the mountain. As we climbed the hill and the steps to the top in the blistering heat, we spoke about my interest in possibly dating a Syrian guy.

"There have been a couple of nice men in my classes but they were all taken. People get engaged so young here." I exhaled, annoyed at how old I was. "Guys here like 'em young!"

"It isn't that easy for a Syrian girl to find a husband either so don't worry. That's why loads of them go to the mosque to ask a sheikh to cast a spell for them." My ears pricked up at the word 'spell' and images of candles, old books and smoke sprang to mind. Sara saw my face and said, laughing,

"Not the kind of spell you do – but similar. They write some words on paper and the girl and her mum recites them together. The mum is always the driving force between that type of thing here. The actual word in Arabic for this translates as spell in English."

"That sounds like a similar spell to what I would have done when I was younger. I don't really do it anymore." I replied.

"Well, yes. They use trinkets and herbs too so it is very similar I guess." Sara continued, sounding curious. "Why don't you cast spells anymore?" I considered it before answering – I wasn't sure myself.

"I don't know really – I haven't really had much of an urge to do it since I was about eighteen. I have done small things since then, which were more for healing as opposed to gaining a physical thing. For instance the sacred marriage I told you about… oh and I do things like write letters to people who have hurt me, thanking them for how what happened actually helped me and then I burn it … in my cauldron!" We laughed at the fact that I actually owned a cauldron and seeing that we were now outside the main door, bowed our heads to fit through the tiny frame and went inside the dark church.

The nuns looked at me – the foreigner - in interest as I watched my friend do some kind of prayer ritual. I didn't know what to do really, so just stood there awkwardly, until I noticed an enormous statue in a corner of the church. It was covered with offerings of fruit and flowers: a bronze interpretation of the lovely Virgin Mary. She was pregnant, one hand on her stomach and looking down in reverence at the growing life inside her. *Isn't that how every woman feels when they are pregnant?* I wondered as I stepped silently towards it, narrowing my eyes in deep, sudden thought. I didn't have any children but I assumed that I would be as emotional about it too.

I mulled over the idea of the *immaculate conception* as I stood there shivering in the shadows of this enormous building. Or was I feeling cold in the shadow of this revered woman who exemplified the very notion of 'purity' – the opposite of how I was viewed in the Middle East. *I wonder what Mary's role in the birth of Jesus actually was* I thought, tilting my head to one side as was my habit when I questioned something. Did the fact that she birthed a baby that was so spiritually perfect mean anything? Did it say anything about her as a woman and her ability to co-create with God to manifest an immaculate concept, in other words a perfect idea? I knew from my spell work and life experience that I seemed to have the ability to manifest things into reality too. *There have been times when I feared something and it came into being and when I wanted something desperately and it happened,* I remembered. But I didn't have time to see where my meditations were leading me because I heard Sara calling my name and I noticed how pretty 'Tina' sounded as it echoed, ringing off of the church walls like bells.

Later Sara and I burnt wishes in the flame of a pink candle. I tried to concentrate but my mind was racing with thoughts of the Mother Mary. Packing up our things under the hot sun, I decided to ask Sara.

"Do you think it is possible to love in a perfect way?" She nodded that yes she did.

"I think I love my boyfriend perfectly because he is everything I have dreamt of. He is a perfect match for me and he makes my heart race. We are the same religion. Our parents will agree to our marriage and he has a good job to support our future family. What could be more perfect than that?" She laughed in her gentle way, her jet-black curly hair, hanging loose from her band swayed in the silence. I noticed her delicate hands as she tied a string around a bunch of light blue taper candles. She was a perfect Syrian girl.

" I suppose so!" I chirped back with a false joviality and in leisurely time. We were both more relaxed up there in the mountains. I was perturbed though. There I was, sitting, praying to the Goddess for love when I wasn't sure I even knew what love was. I was reminded, instantly of David, on my trip in Egypt who had said that the concept of 'specialness' is not conducive to living a happy and peaceful life. But isn't that what we do when we love one person? We single them out as being 'better' than everyone else. People do it all the time – they get a boyfriend or girlfriend and the rest of the world can go to hell! I hadn't cared about anyone else when I was with Ryan. Was that why I was unhappy and alone now?

Thinking of God made me depressed. I was in this country where I was considered a *freak* for not being married in my late twenties and David … and Ryan … come to think of it, had said that relationships were bad according to *A Course in Miracles*. God was confusing me. If relationships were so bad why did everyone around me see them as good? Sara thought her boyfriend would be proposing any day now and she looked like the cat that got the cream. When I got home that evening I rooted around a box I kept some old stuff in.

"So this is where my *Friends* DVDs got to… and my *Paulo Coelho* collection!" I said out loud. They weren't what I was looking for now though. I fished around the box some more until something gold flashed at me under my fluorescent lighting – *yes, here it is*, I thought, lifting out a heavy book I had never even opened. I didn't recall shipping it to Syria but there it was amongst all my stuff: the copy of *A Course in Miracles* that David had given me in Egypt. It freaked me out that the book had managed to hunt me down two thousand miles away back then and it freaked me out now, finding it there with me in Syria, quietly watching me from its dusty old box. I hadn't even known of its existence until I bought it for Ryan that day a year and a half ago but now it seemed to be everywhere I was, chanting things I didn't understand. An image of David possessed by the spirit of the book came to mind and I chuckled, rolling my eyes at myself for being so dramatic. I picked it up with two fingers like it was contagious and took it into my spare room where an old cabinet stood. I left the book there before locking the double doors as if I expected the book might escape by itself, hold me hostage and force me to read it. The book was a trigger for thoughts of *If only Ryan hadn't cheated on me we would still be together now.* I was destined to become a childless, TEFL victim and it was his fault. I promised myself that I would never ever listen to what Jesus had to say. David's words had got to me at the time but now I knew what was best for me. I needed a boyfriend to make me whole and to heal my heart – not a crazy book.

Chapter 22

A couple of weeks later, a tempest blew in. My tower toppled and I watched everything that was mine fly away. My heart and spirit was flung around in a whirlwind until the person I was no longer existed. My idea that love and marriage would be the way toward fitting in and in return somehow 'purify' me, played out in front of my eyes when I was least expecting it.

"Are you feeling better?" Asked Sara, books in front of her and head tilted to one side in concern. She had been covering a class for me whilst I was away with a serious toothache. A Syrian dentist – sounds dodgy – but I told anyone and everyone that they were the best kind. I had had root canal and it took hours for him to remove the nerve causing all the problems. Not quite as humble as the British dentist, he waved it in my face after he extracted it, and its pink legs jangled in the air; him grinning and puffed up. I put my hand to my jaw, remembering and frowned.

"Kind of. How was the class?"

"Oh they were great. We covered everything. But you have a couple new students who enrolled last week." Sara went quiet for a second and pressed her lips together, eyes darting from left to right. I went to reply but instead just stared at her, eyes growing in surprise. The girl was looking around the room as though she were anticipating an attack by the secret police. Just as suddenly, she dove close to my ear. "There's a new guy. He's really, really cute." I smiled and bobbed my head up and down in a slow nod of recognition.

"Ah ha"

"His name is Saleh and… you have to see him!"

Sara dumped her books by a computer and lunged for the door, gesturing for me to follow. I knew she was being discreet because she was a very professional person when in the workplace - one of those paranoid people who think that management has enough time to judge their every move. I was giggling away. I didn't expect much. Syrian guys were hot, but more often than not they were way too short for me. At five foot seven, I was actually considered tall. I was getting ready to ask about his height as we got to the bottom of the staircase when Sara slowed down and said,

"There he is!" I knew immediately without her having to point him out, who it was that had got her all riled up. The most gorgeous man I had ever seen stood at the café, talking with the manager. And he was tall too! I think I literally forgot to breathe for a split second. We both turned around and ran up the stairs, laughing our heads off and generally acting like a pair of twelve year olds.

A couple of days later, I had my first class with him. One minute I was writing a timeline to show the past continuous tense on the white board, the next I was pestering a friend of his for his number. It might be useful to note here that dating a student was not frowned upon as we were mainly teaching adults. I even knew of a few managers and teachers who had ended up marrying students. Later, as I held the piece of paper with Saleh's number on it, I felt sick. I couldn't understand why I was letting myself get caught up in the moment. Sara and I had spent every night on the phone for the past three days, excitedly gabbling on about how he would fall in love with me and propose. Ironically, she said I had the advantage over any other girl because I was a novelty. I was British. All I knew was that I wanted this man like I had never wanted anyone before. He was this thing of complete and utter beauty. His body was muscular and well-defined, shoulders broad and rugby player legs. His facial features were chiseled and the stubble growing around his jaw was divine! I even loved the gruffness in his voice. He was so masculine. I started to see a semblance in the idea I had had about Ryan sleeping with someone he had wanted to *be* because there *was* part of me that wanted to become Saleh. From a distance, he seemed to represent everything a perfect man should be and maybe I wanted to be seen as that perfect woman.

Sara was right though: when I finally called him he did jump at the chance to take me out. We had an awkward dinner on the mountain. I had taken forever to choose what to wear. Black jeans, tight top, heels and a leather jacket, and he stared at me all night, I supposed, not quite believing he was on a date with his teacher. We talked about mundane things and shared family history. His mother had passed away when he was sixteen and his father had married someone else soon after. He told me he hated her and I ummm-ed and ahhhh-ed. He laughed at my attempts to speak Arabic. I encouraged him to speak English. He wasn't as macho as I had first assumed though. He had an immature air to him. Maybe it was because he considered poking fun at people funny and although I couldn't understand the Syrian dialect, his words seemed to be delivered abruptly. Not so much spoken as barked out of his mouth yet I pushed this aside thinking he was nervous. It wasn't the best date I had ever had but I was with him. My yearning for him was overbearing and I slept with him too soon.

"Make sure you wait until he says he loves you or even if his dad gives him permission to marry you," remarked Sara. She became my go-to girl on uncovering the unspoken rules of the Syrian relationship. Alas! I didn't listen and went with my body instead of my logic. It was horrible: uncomfortable and completely meaningless of course. There was an evident separation of body and heart with him - something I had never experienced before but what more could I have expected? In the morning I scolded myself for the lack of common sense approach I had taken. I presumed I really liked this guy. So why didn't I do the obvious thing that Sara had told me would keep him interested? Was primal woman stirring again? It had been a full moon and the rawness of losing myself to him had seemed rooted in the earth and empowering. I sighed. That wasn't the way a good Syrian girl behaved. I had been right about the Goddess getting me into trouble.

"I really, really need to exercise some restraint in the presence of this man! What's wrong with me, I can't believe I did that." Sara's voice was comforting but I knew she was judging me. This time I didn't mind because I deserved it.

"Don't worry. He was probably too young for you anyway. He is five years younger. He's twenty-three. And that is frowned upon in Syria."

"Tell me Sara. Tell me." I said through clenched teeth. "What isn't frowned upon in Syria?"

I felt like a complete idiot. I spent the rest of the day cringing at the memory until it wasn't so much embarrassing as it was confirmation of my unworthiness in this sexually defunct society. I could just imagine what he was telling his friends. He hooked up with his teacher and she turned out to be a typical Brit – up for sex with anyone. But he wasn't anyone to me. He had stirred something within me that even Ryan wouldn't have had a hope in hell of competing with. Now I had lost my chance with him. I had blown it. I didn't want to stare at my phone for the rest of the day, eagerly anticipating texts and calls when he probably would never want to call me again. He had got what he wanted. I ripped the cover off the back of my mobile and pulled out the SIM. I took a pair of scissors and cut it in half. Chucking it into the bin, I looked at it in satisfaction. *Instead of waiting for him to contact me and being devastated when he doesn't, I can save myself the heartache and just, never know.* I sat down on the sofa miserably and tried to forget the whole sorry affair until I heard a car horn going off maniacally downstairs. I opened the sliding doors that led onto my balcony and glanced at my enormous blue jasmine plant. I guessed it had died but now there were little indigo flowers blooming all over it. I was surprised at that but nothing shocked me more than seeing Saleh on the road below in long shorts and a Tee. He had obviously been to one of the many hotel swimming pools littered all over the city. His face had reddened under the harsh Arabic sun but it didn't detract from the beauty that was Saleh. He had thrown his head back and was looking up at me. His eyes penetrated mine with a secret message that only I could understand. He was saying not to worry. That what happened last night was fine. That he still wanted me.

I came undone in the wind; the barriers I had built up around me in Glastonbury and Egypt, unraveling in the strength of it. Now a few months in and our relationship had become brutally honest and unembellished. I liked it at first. It was almost like being two giant magnets being forced to come together. There was a chemical reaction that could not be verbalized or justified. It just was what it was: as natural as one, two, three. Women tend to look for that man who makes their stomach do somersaults. Saleh was the man who did that for me. I could barely eat in his presence, could barely look him in the face in case his beautiful eyes should look back and see some imperfection in me. I was afraid to look at the time because I didn't want him to leave: to live one ounce of his life without me. When he would say goodbye and close the big, white double doors behind him, I would listen to his foot falls on the marble stairs and want to die. When would I see him again? I didn't know but I was aware that I would rather be dead, than live through the unknowing. My attitude shocked me. This was an Arab man I was in love with. *There's no way he's serious*, I would say to Bibi. I questioned my sanity, my feelings and my actions, but Sara comforted me and we continued to make wishes in the mountains: her for marriage; me to be good enough for this man I was convinced was perfect in every way.

I craved to know if I was perfection to him too but he merely swirled between my bed and his life. His inky eyes against his pale skin were devastating. I would have done anything for him. Thick lashes would hide them from me as I looked into them desperately, searching for some feeling or some emotion. I always looked down at my feet, undecided and with tears in my eyes. They were unreadable. Yet behind the breezy confidence, he seemed unsure of himself. Whenever he was shy or embarrassed his cheeks flushed rosy pink. I liked it because it was the only moment I knew what he was feeling. This eventually brought to light my distinct lack of control over where our relationship was going and pushed me even further back to witchcraft and the Goddess. Of course, I didn't work magick to influence his behavior, thoughts or feelings in any way. Life experience had taught me that this was pointless. But I would burn candles and send out positive vibes, building love alters in all corners of my flat.

I gladly forgot David's words. Saleh was special to me and I wanted to be special to him and I fought for that for many months. I physically fought at the expense of my mind, body and soul. My last relationship had been with Ryan. He called me several times a day. He shared his thoughts and feelings with me regularly. He let down his guard and encouraged me to open up to him. Saleh did none of these things and yet we were in a relationship, weren't we? We were sleeping together. I was spending nights on his chest. I cooked for him, celebrated birthdays with him and held hands with him on the dusty streets of Damascus. But he didn't want to hand over his soul to me and I couldn't accept that. He demonstrated this in the harshest way possible. He refused to kiss me. I didn't tell anyone because I wasn't willing to stop fighting for *him*: for *acceptance*. For *redemption* from all the mistakes I had made. For the *cleansing of my spirit*: for *the Goddess to see me as a good person*. Somehow I associated all of these things as qualities that 'pure' Arab women have. If I could just get them to see me in the same way they see each other maybe then I could be *saved*.

I didn't know how much Saleh's rejection would change the very foundation of my being because it was tied in with the rejection I was receiving from other members of this new society I was living in. I didn't know if I wanted Damascus to accept me so that Saleh could or if I wanted Saleh to accept me so that Damascus could. If I went out, men would look at me in ways they didn't look at Syrian women. The ladies would huddle together and leave me on the outside or the opposite - they would invite me into their homes, make me lunch and then gossip about me behind my back, speculating over which Syrian men I was fucking, with the same lips they had used to murmur 'I miss you's and kiss my cheeks. I had thought I was somewhat akin to a feminist before I met Saleh. Before I came to Syria. Now, here I was kneeling at the dick of a man who refused to acknowledge my beating heart. And it was as though I loved him all the more for it because I couldn't pull myself away. All our lives we are told to fight and pursue that which will make us happy. Our teachers told us at school that nothing good in life comes easy and that we have to work hard at things. But isn't it strange to carry on fighting when you know you are losing?

Chapter 23

One day Saleh showed up at my flat and told me to get ready. We were going to his family villa in Saydnaya – the same place where Sara and I visited the church and made wishes in the mountains. I was used to Saleh doing that to me – just randomly barging in (he had a key to my place) and barking orders for me to get ready because he had decided we were going somewhere. I tried to tell him that I was nervous about going but as usual he seemed to look through me, settling down on the sofa to watch *MTV Arabia.* I watched him through my bedroom door roughly push the cushions and throws I had so perfectly arranged on my ornate sofa, down onto the floor as his big body tried to get comfortable on the delicate antique piece.

"Just hurry up!" He ordered, "You take so long to get ready and I haven't got time for that."

As we pulled up, it had just got dark but I could see the house, illuminated by fairy lights draped over walls and lining the garden path from end to end. Saleh had a big grin on his face as I remarked that I had never seen anything like it before. As he took me on a tour, he told me it had been hand built and designed, paid for by his father for his new wife back in the nineties. It had enormous lush green gardens surrounding it, from back to front. There were living spaces designed in an artsy way, with paintings and statues lining the staircases and walls. Saleh said that his father had lived and studied medicine in Germany previously, and looking around at his villa, I could see that he had a cultural flair to him that other Syrians lacked. Probably because he was well travelled too. I found that what separated the tolerant from the intolerant in Arabic countries, were those who had travelled abroad. But then again, isn't that the same everywhere?

As we moved to the outside of the house I heard some American rap music playing at low volume and noticed a group of guys and girls laughing and talking amongst each other. Some were messing around in the pool. A boy, about eighteen years old jumped out in long trunks. He greeted us in English and asked me where I was from. Beer cans were strewn about and cigarette smoke was drifting in the air. Two young teen girls were lounging in patio furniture. Curly hair fell to their waists and they looked at me with dark, jealous eyes. I was, after all, about to steal their focus, in a language they could barely speak.

"Ah! You're from London!" he cried. As I sat down beside Saleh, he moved over to the pool again and stood there, hands clasping the railings of the steps giving me an enormous grin. "But I like America more! It's my dream to go to California!" His English was really good. I muttered something along the lines of sorry to disappoint.

Three other young guys clambered to sit on the edge of the pool. They asked me the usual questions. Why I would want to leave a cool country like England to live in Syria. I answered them good naturedly, even though I could sense the girls' eyes boring into me. One of them started to speak to Saleh in Arabic. I swallowed down instant fury as I could tell she was flirting with him. *Whore*, I thought. Then, Saleh interrupted her by saying that one of the guys was his brother and that I should guess which one. I looked at the two, who were now left by the pool. The others had disappeared inside the house. A bigger built, pale boy with blondish hair and the original loud boy with the friendly face, slim build and dark features. I chose the pale one and was greeted with fits of laughter from all three. Hassan, Saleh's biological brother, was in fact the loud boy who was very opinionated after a few beers and who preferred America to my lovely lion heart England.

Saleh and Hassan looked nothing alike. The next day, when I woke up and Hassan cooked breakfast for me, I realized in personality they were very different too. Hassan was gentle – outgoing and loud, yes but gentle with it. He thought about things which I could sense from what we discussed over tea and eggs and he had layers to him that were on show for everyone to see. He wasn't afraid like Saleh. He didn't feel the need to put anyone down to make himself feel good either. He didn't laugh at me like Saleh did. Instead, he listened to me with interest and respect. I warmed to him immediately and we became great friends.

That summer I spent a lot of time at their villa, in front of their fireplace, when the parents were away in the city. Hassan would tell me stories of his dreams for true love and his dreams to travel. I would make gifts for him to carry to attract true love into his life. Little pouches with rose quartz and rose petals sewed up inside from my own hand especially for him. He was ten years younger than me and I adored his innocence and his dark brown eyes, wide with honesty. I could see his entire soul through those eyes. I could see the universe. I wanted to be his age again. To have a fresh start and look at the world with a heart untainted with disappointment. Sometimes he would invite me out with him and his friends and I would drink with him and hear stories of the latest girl he had given his heart to.

One cold November evening, Saleh took me to the villa to spend the night. We never slept in the same room there. I supposed he thought it would be disrespectful and to that I agreed. I still hadn't met his father and I didn't want our first introduction to be me leaping out of bed in fear and embarrassment. So on that November night, no one was around except Saleh and I, Hassan and their coolest uncle. I didn't know if he *liked me* but he sure as hell liked how I looked. He would ask me how I was.

"Fine, thank you uncle. And you?"

"You are so beautiful today." He would breathe, half a bottle of whisky on his breath. "Ohhh Saleh. She's so beautiful right?" I used to love it when he would say stuff like that because I would notice Saleh sliding over to be closer to me and after a few minutes – he would always wait so as not to be too obvious – put his arm on the back of my chair as though he was claiming me. I *needed* him to acknowledge me. I could be at rock bottom with that man, but one smile, laugh or the most basic touch from him could set me on top of the world. Like with many unhealthy relationships, when things were good it was like being in Heaven but when things turned awry it was hell.

Hassan had been supposed to go out with some friends but he cancelled to hang out with me. The guys got started on a fire because there were no radiators in the villa. I watched Saleh pour petrol on the logs and wrapped my blanket around me. Hassan and I sat right in front of it. It embraced us with light and warmth and I sent a silent prayer of thanks to the energy behind the flames. Fire is an ancient mystery, a canvas for visions past and present. I often enjoyed staring into the flames hoping for mysteries to be revealed to me – like what I had done with the water. I wished to be as wise as those dancing flames.

Hassan was pouring wine when he asked if I wanted to marry Saleh one day. I checked around the room to make sure Saleh was not in hearing range. He wasn't but I merely shrugged my shoulders and looked at the floor. I hated the way I had developed the 'glance down at the floor because I'm not good enough to even consider love in my life' look, which was a result of not quite knowing where I stood with Saleh. When I looked back up again I was relived to see that Hassan had not noticed. He appeared to be entranced by the fire. All I could hear was the crackling of logs and distant beeping of car horns on the main road.

"What do you think your future holds Hassan?" I whispered, not wanting to break the energy that had built up in the room. "Will you marry a Syrian girl and have ten babies?" I sniggered and he feigned shock. His hair was growing upward into a curly afro and it bounced along with his amusement.

"Me? No way. I am not typical Syrian!" We giggled at his attempt to reject these cultural norms and almost looked around the room to see if his grandmother would appear from nowhere to wag her finger at his daring statement. Then just as suddenly he became serious again and looked into the fire as though he knew how to scry too.

"I won't live long." I almost choked on my red wine.

"Shutup! What do you mean?"

The moments that followed seemed frozen in time, like a drawing, immortalized forever on some wall or paper somewhere, as if I knew they would one day haunt me. In them, he is looking at me and he speaks calmly, slowly, as though I must hear every word, every intake of breath: every glimmer of disappointment in his eyes. The way his legs are crossed beneath him. I must remember that: the stubble of his beard and his black, shiny, curly hair. I must hear his accent and the way his lips form the words. It is as though I am being forced to look God in his eyes. I put down my glass to concentrate and he stares into the fire again.

"*Wallahi* it's true," is all he says.

Chapter 24

I loved Saleh and the times we had together and again I made the mistake of telling him too soon. What was wrong with me? It was literally verbal diarrhea. We had just had a little tiff over nothing when I called him to *pour my heart out*.

"I love you."

Silence.

"You… love me?"

"Yes I do." I could literally hear the cogs moving in his mind, slowly whirling, creaking and working to deal with this new information. His long silences spoke volumes and I knew they were saying *err, shouldn't I have said that?* Chatting with Sara that night did nothing to disperse the humiliation.

"If you want a Syrian to marry you, always let him say *I love you* first." She told me breezily, chewing on gum and watching *Arab Pop Idol. I hadn't even told her what I had done yet!*

"Good, God" I groaned down the phone and put my head in my hands. I had baked a bunch of cupcakes for my work colleagues but I was steadily making my way through them. *I am a complete loser.*

"What's wrong?" I heard her ask. I decided I didn't want to relive the incident.

"Oh nothing I had better go now. I need to make cupcakes".

I couldn't get over how much I was sabotaging my own relationship with my 'dream man' and it was obvious I was because he hadn't returned my declaration of love. I was aware of the rules for dealing with Syrian men. Don't have sex with them. Don't tell them you love them until they say it first. Don't call them. Don't text them. Act innocent. *I've broken every bloody one!* I thought in despair. *Maybe these guys were right about me all along. Maybe that horrible Egyptian caretaker was right about me. I am not what a good woman should be.*

On the other hand I did know that the now twenty-four year old Saleh really was just a child, still finding himself. The problem was, I was an adult, feeling pressured into becoming a child again. The expectations of society weighed heavily on my shoulders and nothing reminded me more of that fact than when I met the rest of his family for the first time. They were at the villa for a barbecue and Saleh had permission to bring me along. Hassan and I winked and smiled at each other as I made my way up to through the perfectly manicured lawn – the work of their gardener who maintained the house and land for them. As the villa had been built at a higher altitude than Damascus itself was placed, there was a cool breeze that blew in from the mountains and blustered its way around the garden. Flower petals had succumbed to the wind and were dancing around my feet in white and red hues. I thought that they looked like little whirling dervishes.

"This is Tina, my teacher." Saleh's booming voice broke through my daydream. About twenty faces looked up from their meals to acknowledge my presence and I smiled back. This was it: my last hope. I had exhausted all other avenues that might lead to a marriage proposal. The only one left was to make his family like me. *So he had introduced me as his teacher.* I told myself it could work to my advantage because if he had said I was his girlfriend, they might have immediately assumed that we were in an inappropriate sexual relationship – which of course we were – but letting them think that might not be a good idea in the long run. So I soothed myself with the proposition that it was okay for now. Inside I wallowed in the disappointment that I wouldn't be able to claim him or show others that he belonged to me this evening.

The task of getting his family to like me would be harder than I thought. His father was harsh and abrupt, his little stepsister, distant and moody and his stepmother, cold and rude.

"So do you have any younger sisters?" his father had asked me, after finding out I was going on thirty. Was he implying I was too old to be around his son?

"Yes, two. One is twenty-seven and the other twenty-five now. I don't have any brothers."

"Why are you in Syria? Do you like it?"

"Of course!"

"Why?" his eyes remained fixed on mine, as he took a swig of red wine.

"I like the people and the food and the way of life. It's so different from London."

"Well of course it is different!"

Oh my God, why does this man hate me? I tried to tell myself it was because he was a doctor – he had to have an air of authority about him. He must be like that with everyone. But I knew the answer. I was an inappropriate choice of woman for his son and there was nothing I could do to change that.

I watched his aunts and uncles interact with each other – I couldn't join in because of the language barrier – and I looked at the women in envy. Their perfectly made-up faces and manicured nails portrayed their easy life styles. They knew their place in the world because they had followed 'the rules' of Syrian dating etiquette and had married their dream men. They would never have to go on journeys to *find themselves*. I was everything that was frowned upon in Damascus society. I was an untrustworthy foreigner, I was a few years older than my boyfriend; I was not a bloody virgin! And so there I stood, amidst these people having a family barbecue. Them, mingling and laughing together and me, looking at the man I love so much, knowing that here, I have no value. Glancing at the young women, married or not, I see their worth, and wish I were worth something too.

Over the course of our relationship I knew he didn't love me and that society would state that he *couldn't* love me and for some reason, I often theorized that he didn't have to love me back. I wanted to drift along by his side forever, sensing the Goddess with every word he addressed to me, regardless of whether those words were nice or mean because that's how it felt being with Saleh for me – as though I were in the Goddess's arms. I kept praying for his love because I wanted to be his '*the one*' and if I could have scooped him up and held him close to my chest forever, I would have. I had never before had the urge to possess someone this way and I refused to listen to my intuition that tried to tell me spirits cannot be sucked into glass bottles and corked for all eternity. It seems that when people focus on loving one person, they are not connected to that inner voice.

Later that week I was dusting my windowsills. Yellow sand had gathered in the corners and I was just brushing it away with a cloth when an idea popped into my mind. I picked up my mobile and dialed a familiar number. I really hadn't thought this through.

"I have something to tell you." I announced into the phone. "I didn't tell you before because... I guess I was too shy." I heard Saleh shuffle some papers in the background. "Are you listening?" I said, frustrated. This was important. This would change everything.

"Yeah."

"Great so... what I wanted to say is that when we first had sex... I was a virgin." I held my breath and waited for the game-changing response. If anything could make me wifey material it would be this.

"Oh... sorry if I hurt you."

"Err it's okay. Yeah it did hurt a bit but it's fine... errr you didn't know." *Alright* I thought. Not quite the response I had anticipated but Saleh isn't exactly an expressive guy. *Maybe he just doesn't know what else to say. Well at least I had planted the seed.* He said he had to finish some work and we hung up. I stared at the phone. *Any minute now* I told myself, *I am going to get a declaration of his love for me.* As far as he now knew, I had been 'pure' and innocent and no man had touched me before him. If he asked, I could explain away all the inconsistencies.

The declaration never came and nothing changed. In fact we never brought up the subject again. Yes I had lied and that was wrong but I realized afterwards that it was a fruitless lie because I had slept with him out of wedlock and in Syria that makes a woman as good marriage material as a five-dollar hooker. Later, I was not only ashamed of the lie I told but I was ashamed for brushing-off the Goddess within me who is so intertwined with the feminine form and female sexuality. I realized I shouldn't have been seeing myself as *only a woman* but as a vessel for the Goddess herself according to our old tradition. Even well known tools of the average witch, such as her cauldron, are in fact yonic symbols and are an expression of the sacred nature of sex. After all what is not divine about the means by which children are brought into the world? I denied myself her power – my own sexual power – and laid it at the feet of a man who saw it as worthless filth. Nevertheless, at that moment in time, in the midst of my spiraling depression, it was a stab in the dark and a last ditch attempt to capture his heart.

Chapter 25

Why is it that emotional breakdowns always seem to happen in a bathroom? Maybe it's because it's where the water in a house, typically lives and flows and in witchcraft, water represents emotion. After a fourth break up with Saleh and over a year in, I found myself on the edge of madness. I probably looked mad too, in my long, white silky nightgown, stained with tears and makeup. My jade ring from the sacred marriage ceremony had been flung into a corner in frustration. It didn't seem right to wear it anymore. I was certain I had let myself down. I had fallen in love and lost control of everything.

I couldn't even remember what our fight was about or why I had demanded he return my key. Ironically it was the action I had taken due to me not being familiar with Syrian culture and custom that had ended our relationship. I essentially committed a cultural faux pas that involved the kicking of his backside out of my house. He had done something or other to offend me, but how was I to know that ejecting a man from your home in Syria means he can hold it against you for the rest of your life? I had never had to kick Ryan out, but I may have at some point and I didn't think it would be considered such a big deal. We both spend the night angry, but make peace the next day. *No big deal, right?* I had said to myself. I inhaled and sighed out loud until my breath ran out. *My concerns about being at a disadvantage because I wasn't an Arab were legitimate after all.*

Saleh had come to the house, voice grave, stating that I had deeply offended him. He was trying to make me understand I hurt him or hurt his ego – I didn't know which one.

"In Syria this is a very bad thing to do. You told me to leave your house." He said. "Now I am leaving and you will never see me again." I listened to him and his calm nature fooled me into thinking he wasn't serious. I had never seen him shout at anyone before. I liked that about him.

"Well how the hell was I supposed to know that? I am sorry. I didn't mean it." I bent down to stroke our cat – a birthday gift from him to me. We were standing in my hallway. A picture of *Kahlil Gibran* had pride of place on the wall and potted plants boasted emerald leaves that climbed and climbed until they hung upside down from the ceiling. I started rearranging a couple when I heard him go for the door.

"What? Where are you going?"

"Bye Tina." He was unlocking it now and I grabbed him by the hand.

"Saleh, please." Desperation was creeping into my voice. I didn't recognize myself. “I’m sorry. I don't know about all these Syrian rules. If I had I wouldn't have disrespected you in that way.” I pulled him back inside and made him sit on the sofa. Its Bedouin throw sank down and cushions scattered on the floor. “Please don't leave me Saleh. It was a mistake.”

“It’s over. Don't call me again,” he stated firmly. To my surprise, he looked upset and resigned but he had never tried hard enough. How dare he act like *he* was tired of *me*. Tired is when you keep trying and get nowhere. Tired is when you are out of options. *He* was the one who made me feel like filth when he dodged my kisses, *he* was the one who never called. He went to go for the door again. I grabbed the sides of his head in my two hands and gently pulled him close, forehead against forehead we were. As if I could transfer my thoughts into his head, thoughts of togetherness and love and passion, forever.

“I’m sorry. Please forgive me.”

“No.” was all he said. I let go of him in slow motion. I didn't want to though. I wanted to shake his head in my hands until his terrible thoughts about me dispersed. I was sick of not being good enough and I was sick of those degrading opinions he seemed to hold about me that were so dear to him. It didn't occur to me that they might be my own. So I let him go. But now I can't function with the guilt. Instead I lie on the cool marble floor. I am so tired of this. So tired of crying and feeling insecure and analyzing over and over again, why Saleh can't at least *pretend* he can give me more. He hadn't said he loved me, he was aloof and out of contact with me for long periods of time. That is not the approach of a man who is taking a relationship seriously. To make matters worse, Sara told me that meeting his family means nothing and that Syrian men take friends home to their parents all the time.

I am conscious of being drowsy and close my eyes to the cruel images that haunt me: Saleh with another girl, Saleh's father asking about my younger sisters, Saleh laughing at me with his friends and then, I think I am drifting off to sleep because I am back in Egypt now and standing in a pure, white desert. I don't know this place by sight, but it sounds familiar in a way. I look down at myself, notice I am wearing a dress the color of Lapis Lazuli and mesmerized by its otherworldliness, I lift my arms up to dance with my shadow on the sand. Yellow gold bracelets twinkle on my wrists and ankles and I assume the sun must be blaringly hot today but I am barefoot and it is blissfully cool as I dig my toes in sand. There is something odd about this desert though. I look about me as I move but the bright, white light keeps me from seeing too far ahead so I stop and brace myself to listen out for the sound of a road or people but I am surrounded by stillness and as I glide into it, I lose all memory of where I am supposed to be. *I am here and I have always been here.*

It is then that I see the circle: an infinite circle of people where everyone is holding hands and none is more important than the others. I look at their faces but they seem to blend in with their neighbor's and have no distinctive features. They are merely a harmony of color and feeling. The peace swirls round and round and the people share the joy that I feel is … 'God' with each other in that circle. I am closing my eyes in awe and wonder at these enlightened ones when, quick as a bolt of lightening, I am thrown at the foot of a great temple standing in another vast Egyptian desert and I wonder how it could have arisen out of such serenity.

Amidst the cacophony of wailing and jeering, there were builders and people managing the builders and people instructing the managers and I know they are the people from the circle but they weren't holding hands anymore and they barely remembered the peace of this God energy. They were too busy determining that they can be rich or poor, beautiful or ugly, special or not and I realized I was witnessing the birth of civilization in the construction of those temples. I was being shown how the Ego was born. The temples stood there, harsh and rooted in the world with the same ability to judge a person, worthy or unworthy. I was sensing the battle between the mountains and the temples, like I had on the spiritual tour of Egypt I did with Bob, and it took me right back to the war inside myself once more.

I open my eyes to find myself back on my icy floor. I was sure I had been awoken by the sound of something dropping to the ground.

"Saleh?" I call but the abrupt beginning of an Azan drowns my weakened voice out. "The mosque didn't wake me." I say to myself rising to my feet. "It was a thud coming from inside the house." I start opening the doors to each room, searching for anything that may have produced that noise. I rub my forehead, as the singing from the mosque appears to get louder and try to erase memories of the strange dream I had. When I get to the doors of the spare room, something makes me hesitate but I push ahead anyway and throw them open. I gasp in fear and it takes all the strength I have not to run away. Lying on the floor is *A Course in Miracles*. A shiver runs down my spine as I close the doors, never taking my eyes off the book. I know I can't ignore it this time. I mutter random questions aloud, trying to understand. "Is God really there? I suppose he must be laughing at me. Is that what Magda was doing at the end of my bed that day? Laughing at me for how stupid I am? Well if you hate me so much God, you change me! You have the power don't you?" I waited for a second, for God's staff to strike me with enlightenment from the heavens – for this God figure to magically transform me into a better person. I waited for a few more minutes before staggering to the bathroom, not quite knowing why it drew me there. I had never cried in the bathroom before and I had spent a lot of time *releasing* in that house.

"God, Jesus, whoever you are, please help me." I envision my guardian angel and call to her too. I pray with such conviction that it echoes around the room. My fists clench, not in anger but with an energy I thought I had lost years ago. My body is rigid as I chant.

"Come here Magda. Please. Please. Please. Come here now. I need you. I need you. Just, please, come here."

It was reciting a spell to conjure a spirit; it was an affirmation of belief, an attempt to find my way back home. I knew she would come to me – she had to – I was in so much pain. This conviction that my angel who I first 'met' sitting on the end of my bed would appear, swelled and swelled until I was practically spitting out the words. Not in a violent fashion but in a manner that was so energized, I imagined sparks flying out of my palms. Magda is my guide and will be with me through thick and thin. I know it. My cries are surely bouncing off of the trees in the broken-down house below. They are bellowing over the rooftop. And then my tone lowers and I am speaking and I am asking Magda to help me, steadily sounding out the words – anticipating them and forming them. Until, I find myself whispering: my voice slow and methodical, almost rhythmic with intention until only my lips are moving. It is then that my heart speaks the words. Each beat, like a primitive drum. Like the beat echoing off the walls of the

Great Pyramid. It speaks for me in a voice born before the beginning of time.

Chapter 26

But Magda didn't come to me that afternoon. Instead, I got a text from Sara inviting me round for dinner so I decided to gather my composure and head round there. Sara always gave great advice so I planned to go over with her what I should do next and I felt sure it involved leaving my work contract a few weeks earlier than the initial two years. I had let myself get carried away with Saleh and I needed to go home. I was clearly not coping. I was a mess and all because of a *guy?* And what was all that bullshit about God that I had been spewing? That cabinet was full to the brim – the course must have just been expelled out of its cramped shelf by other falling books.

Sara had just returned from London and had a lot of photos to show and stories to tell. The main purpose of the trip had been to get some training provided by the British school but she had made the most of her time away. As we settled at her rocky kitchen table, She poured out her specialty – black tea with a pinch of cinnamon. We laughed over a few pictures of her doing funny poses and I caught her up on the gossip at work. Many of our colleagues had finished their contracts and had gone to other schools around the world. This was definitely a factor that contributed to my depression as I was becoming lonelier in Damascus. I had no distraction during the days Saleh disappeared and was out of contact with me and I genuinely missed the good friends I had made, especially Bibi who had moved to Dubai. As I was explaining this to her, she and I grabbed some biscuits and more tea and headed to the living room to get comfy on the sofa when a strange atmosphere seemed to come over the room. Things were moving in slow motion, the most minor actions grabbing my attention. I knew something was stirring. I kept quiet. Sara said,

"A new girl is coming next week so I don't think work will be that boring anymore. I think you might like her. You guys could hang out maybe." I looked at her in interest. Her spoon dripped tea onto the coffee table.

"I met her on the course in London."

"Wow! That's a coincidence! Is she nice?" I asked, wondering if I should wipe up the spilled tea with my tissue. I still felt a bit off and so I decided to stay where I was. Moving might break the energy.

"Yeah – she actually wasn't doing the course. She teaches at the college and yeah… she's okay. A little bit strange I guess." She went on to explain that the girl was quite open and shared a lot of intimate details about herself in the space of a half hour lunch break and that she probably wouldn't be befriending her. She looked disgusted as she relived a point in the conversation when the girl had asked whether she should bring condoms with her. As sweet as Sara was, she could be quite judgmental, and the smallest things could put her off people for life. I supposed it was quite forward to ask such a question but she is British. We can be a random bunch at times. I didn't say much. Instead I sipped tea and listened, feeling cold. Winters in Damascus could get *really* cold. As she spoke, I assumed that this new person would be older and would come with a family or a partner, but Sara said she was single and our age. Now I was very interested! Someone I could get close to maybe? Hang out with? Show the ropes? At this point in time I was the foreign teacher who had been at the school the longest.

"What's her name?" Sara picked up a biscuit. It looked good: thick chocolate with a dusting of coconut. I watched as the coconut snowed in slow motion onto the carpet. She creased her forehead in a display of 'I don't remember' and looked up at the ceiling.

"Ah. Yes. I know. It was Magda."

Silence.

Magda.

Flashes of me, not four hours ago on my bathroom floor, crying out for

God to send me Magda – my angel – for comfort, appeared before my eyes. I couldn't speak. Instead I just stared at my friend shoving the chocolatey goodness into her mouth and in the dragging moment, her face seemed etched in stone as she looked back at me realizing she had said something meaningful. Mid-chew I think she asked if I was okay and I must have nodded. I tried to think of something to say. Tried to respond. Didn't know if I should explain my strange reaction or not. I chose not to. Instead I asked what Magda looked like.

"Blonde hair. Blue eyes. I think she said she is originally Polish or something." I honestly couldn't believe it.

Calling the appearance of a 'Magda' into my life a 'coincidence' would be just plain lazy. It was as though I had pulled her into my reality. I watched the new teacher a couple of weeks later, on her induction with the manager at work out of the corner of my eye, trying not to stare. I suppose I was looking for something that made her angel-like. She looked pretty human to me. *Does she recognize me?* I tried to catch her attention. *No... and now she looks a bit freaked out. I'd better stop staring like a serial killer.*

This wasn't like any spell I had ever cast in my life. I hadn't lit any candles or burned any incense. *All I had done was... pray?* But that's what Christian people do... *who had heard me and answered?* I wondered. And the idea that God may have helped me entered my mind for the first time in my life. God. The God that belonged to David and Ryan had answered my call for help? A memory came back to me of a conversation between my ex and I over the phone. I was upset that I hadn't been able to find a teaching job and so Ryan suggested this night, before we went to sleep, that we pray and ask for a job to come to me, together. I listened intently as he asked God for the right position to open up and I said

"Amen," when he was done. I had never prayed before and didn't know how. When I woke up the next morning I found a text message on my phone from a manager I had never met, asking if I could go for an interview. An acquaintance of mine had passed my details on to him as she wanted to leave her teaching post in his department and he would require a replacement. It turned out to be the break I needed and I worked there for many years to come but I tried never to think of this experience. It was so alien to what I was used to and too many implications arose. Especially thoughts of 'why me?' I am a witch – the Bible says God hates me so why would I be granted a prayer? It didn't make sense. But this time was different. Similar to the book falling to the floor by itself, the Magda incident was too strange to push aside and I decided I needed to discover the truth.

First, I got Sara to take me to a bookshop and help me choose a Bible. I bought it, took it home and immediately opened it up to the part of the story I was most interested in: Mary is visited by an angel, who informs her that she is to become pregnant with the savior of the world.

'Behold the handmaid of the Lord; be it unto me according to thy word.' She had replied.

I pondered over this for many days. Mary had manifested something into her life, so miraculous, which in turn brought her so close to God that she changed the very course of the world. And all because she had made the choice to surrender her will to the Divine, which ultimately means that she chose to trust God with her life. *Maybe doing so gave her the power to be able to see through His eyes?* I thought. Maybe that's why she was able to birth Jesus – a man who brought peace, love and light to the world – because she *chose* to be in tune with the energy of the Divine.

Mary chose not to fight God despite all that she might have lost as a pregnant, unwed woman living in those times, yet the realization that I was doing the opposite hit me so hard, I almost fell to the ground with the pain of it. If I had really found the Divine I would be overwhelmed with peace and joy but instead I had climbed over my balcony railings a few times and hung there, praying for death and a way out of what I was seeing as my reality. I had been so alone and so convinced that I was unworthy, but now because of my answered prayer, I had a new friend called Magda who turned out to be a shining light in my dark days. I did befriend her and she remains in my life even now. As much as I loved the Goddess and the power of nature, I had a calling elsewhere and I was now willing to answer.

I crept up to my spare room. It was a sunny day. White light was streaming into it and was almost blinding as I reached for the handles. Radiance leaked through the glass panels on the doors but I pushed them open anyway and stepped into the stuffy space. It was boiling hot. I needed fresh air so I heaved a sliding window upwards and then looked down on the ground, hoping it was where I had left it. It was and I got on my knees to have a closer look. I ran my finger over the spine; the indigo cover had noticeably dulled but other than that it was perfectly readable. I had no more excuses. With one swift movement I threw open the front cover. A few of the first pages went with it in my haste, leading me straight to the introduction. The paragraph I was greeted with held more magick for me at that time in my life than any midnight frolic in the woods or scrying session in dark waters. It spoke of the goal of the Course, as being to remove barriers to love's presence within us.

"The opposite of love is fear, but what is all-encompassing can have no opposite. This course can therefore be summed up very simply in this way: Nothing real can be threatened. Nothing unreal exists. Herein lies the peace of God."

I thought it sounded like a very beautiful riddle that I wanted to commit a lifetime to solving. I held the book to my chest. It emitted an aura so peaceful that I thanked it in gratitude and this, I can say, was the beginning of my dialogue with *A Course in Miracles.*

Chapter 27

Despite falling in love with the language and ideas in A Course in Miracles, I felt somewhat distanced from the possibility that I – your average girl who grew up on an East London council estate, could live in such a way. I understood why Ryan had loved the book so much. It is brimming with the promise of peace and joy and exercises to eradicate all the negative thought processes our society has been hosting for so long. But not only that – the brother Jesus figure speaks so eloquently to the human heart and is so loving that it is impossible to read the book and feel alone, so much so, that the text itself becomes a companion. It is flexible too, for a person who may come from any spiritual background as I do because it can be read religiously or simply as a course that conditions you to think more loving, peaceful thoughts. All it takes is an open mind and the information within is accessible. However, often I felt that the content was so perfect it couldn't possibly apply to me. Plus, I had already lived out my Syrian-Egyptian adventure and was heading back to boring London. Why had I felt the urge to open this book with all the answers, right at the end of my spiritual journey? It didn't make sense.

We were in a bar with a few of his friends when I told Hassan I would be leaving Syria.

"I'm going back home." The music was blaringly loud and the lighting was dim. I looked down at my purple cocktail and thought it was pretty. It reminded me of an amethyst crystal as light bounced through it and I clasped it tighter. Vodka had healing powers too. It had been a couple of months since the breakdown in the bathroom and I hadn't seen Saleh since. Magda – my colleague and part time angel or so I was convinced – had been staying with me while she looked for a place of her own and she *had* kept my mind off of him. I was teaching her all about Syria. How to deal with the men, how to behave in a taxi, who she should consider renting a place from, there was a lot to learn.

"But why can't I live with that man?" She had complained after falling in love with an Arabic house in Sarooja, an area in central Damascus. She brushed her shiny yellow hair out of her eyes and huffed and puffed at me.

"This is Syria. It's inappropriate for you to live alone with a married man." I tried to be calm and understanding. "I know you love the house but you are not going to be comfortable there. I just know it."

"But I am a British citizen and the school can help me out. Surely the rules don't apply for me."

I closed my eyes for what seemed like a long time and watched the movie of horrors play out before me. The caretaker, the guys on the street I had problems with. It all came screaming back.

"Magda. There's no way on this Earth I am allowing you to live in a house with a weird man who is married but says his wife lives somewhere else!" I was talking a million miles an hour. I did not want this girl to go through hell like I had in trying to understand Arabic custom and culture. "Learn from my mistakes and experiences Magda, please, or everything I have been through would be pointless." She sat back on my sofa and looked resigned.

"Go on."

"I have a bad feeling that's all. Sara agrees with me. She is Syrian. She knows how it works here and she says it is inappropriate and that you would be putting yourself in an awkward situation." Magda's blue eyes seemed to twinkle green and gold in the bright sunshine streaming in through the open balcony doors. My floor length curtains filled with the breeze, white and wispy. I waited for her response.

"Okay, okay. Come with me tomorrow to look at the flat down the road?"

I breathed a sigh of relief when she agreed to take that place. Not only because we could hang out everyday but because I was so pleased that my bad experiences could be put to good use. I had invited her to the bar with Hassan and I, but she was home packing. Something I needed to start doing too.

Glancing at him, I didn't think he had heard my announcement the first time because he was laughing with a guy sitting next to him.

"Hassan. I said I'm going home." I grinned as I noticed he and his friend had spied a cute girl. I poked him and watched as he took a swig of his vodka and coke.

"She winked at me ya know."

Everyone around the table started slapping him on the back and making jokes in Arabic. I liked hanging out with Hassan. His friends had a good vibe. He turned to look at me and lowered his voice. Shaking his head he said,

"Is this about my brother because if it is he's stupid. He's just so stupid." His face contorted as he freed the rush of words and my stomach lurched. I had never seen Hassan angry before. I knew what he meant immediately. I had known all along that Saleh had not been shy in admitting he was not serious about me – to everyone *but* me.

"I mean, if I mean nothing to him, why has he continued seeing me for the past – what has it been now? A year and a half? Anyway, that's not the point. We aren't together anymore. It has been hard but I know I can deal with it. I just need a break." I clenched my teeth in frustration at the whole situation. "I know it's my fault really. But my Syrian friend encouraged me. She must have known all along that he and I didn't have a future."

"I am sure she was only trying to help." He soothed. Hassan saw the best in everyone.

I pushed my amethyst drink away and almost knocked it over in the process. Nausea was rising in the back of my throat. This was why I had never asked Saleh straight up, why he was often out of contact with me. Or why he gave the impression that he didn't care. It hurt too much to know and now his brother had confirmed it. Hassan was staring down at his own glass as though he were deep in thought.

"You can do better than him." He said finally. "I don't know why he acts this way. He acts like an oaf. Not all Syrian men act like that. You can find someone else here Tina."

I pursed my lips and looked past him. Perfect Syrian girls were dancing an elegant belly dance to American hip-hop.

"Come on Tina don't be upset. Maybe it would be good for you to go home after all. I don't want you to go but if Saleh is affecting you like this, it isn't good for you."

I took a deep breath. Hassan's hand was on mine and there was concern in his eyes. I managed a smile.

“I had a meeting with my manager and was really honest and told her I am too depressed to continue the last few weeks at work. Normally everyone is scared of her but she has always been okay with me.” Hassan was looking at me, his usually smiley eyes conveyed regret and worry and friendship. I continued, “So she said that it was fine for me to leave. They have three new teachers lined up anyway.”

“That’s great. Don't worry. Everything will be okay. Go back to England. Relax. And if you ever want to come back, I will be waiting for you! Do you want me to take the cat? He can live at Saydnaya and run around in the wild!”

I laughed and said I would much prefer him to take care of it, as opposed to *rough* Saleh whose good natured attempts to play with animals had them cowering in fear. Hassan turned away to chat to his friends and I caught my reflection in one of the mirrors that lined the walls. I realized why he was so concerned about me. I didn't know I had been crying.

A few days later, Hassan came to pick up the cat Saleh had given me for my birthday the year before. He was the only cat I had ever had – and I had owned a lot – that used to literally jump into my arms when I got home from a long day at work. He was tabby with chunky paws. Once, he fell in the toilet and I only realized in the morning when his long hair looked fluffier than usual and the toilet water was a strange shade of brown.

Hassan had been playing basketball on the grass and it had rained the night before. He was trudging through my spotless apartment leaving a trail of footprints and I was chasing after him with a mop. Tomorrow it would no longer belong to me but I still couldn't bear to leave a mess – my Virgo side coming out.

"Don't Syrians take off their shoes before they enter a home? Turks do. My dad is always telling us to take our shoes off." He was at the fridge now. He was so tall I may as well have been in conversation with his behind. It replied,

"Nah we don't do that here." I stopped mopping and waited for him to turn around, head cocked to the right, eyebrows raised.

"Take your bloody shoes off man!" He put one of my homemade pancakes into his mouth so half of it was hanging out, and flung his trainers off.

"Happy?"

"Very!" He grinned cheekily, his handsome face conveyed such gentleness and innocence, and then he remembered and his face fell. I took a deep breath. I had been trying to block it out too.

"Is he ready then? I am so sorry I can't stay but I have a lift back to Saydnaya with a friend and he will be downstairs in literally five minutes."

"Yes, yes of course. I understand." I hurriedly ran to get the cat carrier from the other side of the house and laid it on my dining room table. The walk to get the cat that was sleeping on my bed seemed to take forever, as though my feet were sinking in quick sand. It took all the strength I had to pick him up, kiss his furry head and put him in the cage. Hassan had his trainers back on and was on the phone with his friend. He took my angel and I mouthed a goodbye through little plastic bars. Hassan balanced his phone on his shoulder freeing up one arm to hug me with.

"Bye Tina. Please take care. Please forget about Saleh. Stay in touch with me. Come back to visit soon." I just hugged him back, emotionless, like a robot, said okay and heard his footfalls on the marble staircase.

If I had known what would happen, if I had guessed, I would have grabbed Hassan and begged him not to go. I would have said there was no rush. Stay here with me and let me talk with you, dance with you; sing with you. I want to laugh together and cry together and howl louder than we've ever howled before. I would have said let's go to Palmyra and walk between the ancient stones that lie there and let's hug. Let's embrace tighter still. We would stay together in that moment, just you and me. Then I would hold your hand under lady moon – your beautiful hand – and read you poetry that spoke of love for God and reverence for nature and uplifted mankind. I would do with you, absolutely anything that would make our final parting moments less mundane.

Chapter 28

Later that evening I met up with a student who wanted to have coffee before I left. We walked down a busy Damascene road, eating ice cream from takeaway tubs and reminisced about our classes together. I had always been the kind of teacher who made an effort with getting to know students, especially as many institutions value providing a good 'customer service' experience. They were paying for their classes after all, but I didn't mind. It didn't bother me too much. Some of them were very interesting people and our topic of conversation this particular night, quickly turned a little deeper.

"I can't believe what's happening in Tunisia and Egypt, can you?" I asked. "Do you think there would ever be a revolution here?" I made sure to check there was nobody around to overhear. I was still paranoid about the not-so-secret police.

"I wouldn't want it to." I nodded and thought for a second.

"But don't you think it would be nice to live in a democratic country?"

She abruptly stopped walking, and for a second I was afraid I had offended her.

"Look. The Syrian people; they don't know what they want. We are used to being led. These people," She gestured with the flick of her head to a random gathering outside a pizza place, "They have never had the chance to choose a leader, so how will they know what is good for them? They don't. You can't just cry out *revolution for the oppressed Arabs!* From the comfort of your Western living rooms, parroting from the Western media and using minds shaped from a Western education system. British people, American people – you lot have no clue about our society and yet you think you know what is best for us."

As she spooned more ice cream into her mouth, I considered this idea and wondered how many people thought that way. This girl was highly educated and had an excellent career with a good family background. She was obviously critically examining the underlying issues involved and it impressed me. I had been led to believe that the Syrian education system did not value this skill highly enough to include it in their curriculum and again I thought of my dad fleeing Turkey. They had attempted to kill off the students – people who were learning how to think critically about everything, including politics. I hoped they wouldn't do that in Syria.

"Assad has done this country good. Look at how our tourist industry has grown! Many of my friends and family don't want the chaos a so-called revolution might bring so I am really, really hoping these rumors I'm hearing aren't true."

"What rumors?"

"That we are going to have a revolution." She mouthed 'revolution' and my heart skipped a beat. "A few of my colleagues – a couple of friends - they are calling for revolution Tina. My view is just my view. Some idiots really do want this."

Her words haunted me as I set off for the long walk to the cinema in the city center. I had to agree that I couldn't imagine a revolution in Syria either. Protesting was not only risky for one person. It would put entire families and communities at risk of backlash from the police. People who wanted to save their own skins would no doubt end up reporting others and the result would be a never-ending cycle of finger pointing. It just seemed to be such an unlikely possibility that I couldn't get my head around it. Instead I thought about never seeing my friends at the school again. They had organized a leaving party for me and I could see I was going to be late. But I took my time anyway. This was probably the last time I would set foot on this road again. I would never see that building again or smell the desert sand in the air again. I had become used to Syria but I wasn't used to the people yet, who had thus far, refused to accept me. I couldn't imagine shunning a person in the street in London, based on where they were from. Learning the word for foreigner, good naturedly taught to me by a colleague in my last few weeks in Damascus, only served to make me realize that fitting in there was impossible. I would always be the *ajnobia.* I heard the word chanted a thousand times, everywhere I went in the space of twenty days. Buying fruit, *ajnobia.* Walking through the park, *ajnobia.* Looking into shop windows, *ajnobia.* I knew it was probably their curiosity but at low points it sounded like hissing and spitting. They were telling me to go home but I had been like a naïve child who kept running back for more.

Saying goodbye to everyone at the party was sad, going home alone to sleep in my house without my cat was terrible and not hearing from Saleh, despite him knowing I was leaving was devastating. We had shared so much together. But he had told me to leave him alone and I respected his wish. Although I am not one to believe in fairytales, I did wait to see if he would appear under my balcony. It was four in the morning when I realized he wasn't coming. I looked around me at the remnants of my pathetic life stuffed into several cardboard boxes and had to acknowledge that although I had lived in a flat that was the envy of all my friends and colleagues, it hadn't brought me the happiness I thought it would. In fact I had grown to hate it because it was merely a distraction that kept me in a state of forgetting. I had forgotten who I was and I had forgotten the Divine. I hadn't used my home for a true purpose. It was now like a house of mirrors from a carnival; everywhere I looked a distorted reality was thrown back at me and I had spent two years lapping it up. I hated myself for that weakness, knowing I had *A Course in Miracles* to consult the whole time but was too stubborn to read it.

In my despair, and still in my jeans and earrings, I had fallen asleep in the middle of devouring another chapter and lesson from the book and now I am dreaming with the mind of God. I hear echoes of tip of the tongue memories,

"You think you hold against your brother what he has done to you. But what you really blame him for is what you did to him. It is not his past but yours you hold against him." But I don't quite understand. I see Ryan's face in shadow yet I can't figure out why he looks so … *perfect*. Another voice calls out into darkness,

"You must learn to see them as they are and understand they belong to God as you do." I try to catch a glimpse of the person talking, but there is just a deep blackness – a calm stillness that stretches for miles. A vision forms in front of me. It is Sara, there's Bibi and I see one of my students and I am very aware of my heartbeat now as I see the Egyptian caretaker. My hand moves without me thinking about it and I see myself reaching for his, but before I can clasp it, I am thrown into a bright room filled with a pure, white light. The following reverberates through me,

"Only perfect love exists. If there is fear, It produces a state that does not exist," and I stop trying to comprehend, instead choosing to close my eyes to soak it in. When I open them again I am in my bed and positioned under a cascade of silvery moonlight streaming in through my windows. Amazed by the significance of my dream, I fall to my knees and converse with God in a frenzied prayer of readiness for the next stage of my spiritual quest. I told Him I was ready to abide by Him and that I wanted to understand the true meaning of life and love. I asked Him to use me to fulfill His will in any way He felt fit. I wasn't afraid. I was leaving Syria the next day the same way I had entered: with nothing. I didn't have Saleh and to me that would have been everything. Nursing a broken heart, I *believed* I had nothing to lose.

Chapter 29

"You must learn to end the wars in your world by ending them in your minds."

Barbara Marciniak

Oct. 2011

It had been a summer of skimpy dresses and generous slices of my homemade sponge in vibrant green parks filled with bustling people. This was London at its best and it was full of life so when Death showed up I wasn't able to comprehend that it was truly he who was standing before me now. I kicked and screamed at him and told him firmly that we hadn't requested his presence and to go back to where he had come from but it seemed he did not hear me. When I finally understood that it really was Death and that he wasn't going to budge, I asked why he had to take him. He just looked me dead in the face and told me he was there for me too.

I had returned to London from Syria not too long ago and it was lucky I had permission to leave when I did because just a couple of weeks after my departure, my old colleagues had to be evacuated back home due to what the media claimed, was a revolution kicking off. There was violence in Hama and Homs and a couple of attempts at protests in Damascus so it wasn't looking good but everyone hoped it was just the media exaggerating the whole Arab spring situation that had erupted that year.

I kept in touch with old students and good friends via social media and we updated each other on the latest news so this day was no different. After reading another post by a friend calling for peace in Syria and practicing my lesson for the day from *A Course in Miracles,* I went to make a cup of tea.

“There is no will but God’s, there is no will but God’s, there is no will but God’s.”

My parents had hired a man to insulate the attic and he was banging away above me as I slumped onto my bed, sipping the brew and scrolling through the home page. This time, there was no slowing down of movement around me. Nothing became more defined or called for my awareness, but what I saw on my computer screen would stay in my memory until the day I cease to exist in body and mind. One by one, they popped up in my newsfeed. My eyes were stuck fast to the laptop and so I carefully put the cup down onto the floor, without looking. I didn't realize my lips were parted in shock and horror until I felt my mouth drying up. People were posting pictures of Hassan, Saleh's brother, my beautiful Hassan. He was smiling through them, but they were dark, like he was standing amongst shadows. His excitable puppy eyes were dulled against this photo-shopped image. Above his head, someone had written, 'RIP Hassan'. The words 'Rest in Peace' flooded my newsfeed all of an instant and those words were next to *his* picture. *What were they doing there?* I thought. Why are people saying he should *rest in peace?* He had only just returned from a holiday in Bulgaria. We had spoken a few days ago and in devastating irony my last words to him had been "You're going to be someone amazing in your future." I didn't believe this was true. It couldn't be true. And then I found the page dedicated to him that had been set up over night. I read the information. I saw the words 'shot by soldiers', 'side of the road', 'bullet in head' and I had to muffle my cries with my hands. I didn't want the man upstairs to hear me. I picked up the phone and dialed Saleh's number. We had only spoken twice in the months since I had been back in London. I hoped he hadn't changed his number. My breathing was loud and heavy as I tried to contain everything that I thought I had been holding in for a lifetime, but it must only have been three minutes at the most. As he answered the phone, I wasn't ready for what I heard on the other end and if I could have gone back in time to erase those sounds and images from my mind, selfishly I would.

“Is it true?”

I needn’t have asked. I heard it all down the phone: the music, the people and the wailing. He was at the funeral. Muslims bury their dead the next day. He was being given a martyr’s funeral in his hometown. He paused a long while before answering what I already knew, as if he wanted me to share in his pain, to experience his pain for that fleeting moment.

“Yes.” Then I was almost looking at myself, from the outside, because before my brain had the chance to react, my body was convulsing in tears. I was crying but I didn't understand how I had started to cry without thinking about it first. Things were becoming disjointed so I reached out for my flailing emotions and clutched them back, snapping them onto me like magnets on a fridge. I allowed reason to take over and apologized to him. I couldn't just fling my emotions around when he was dealing with his own. It was his brother, I had to be strong and lessen his pain somehow. I said I would call him back and hung up the phone.

I changed into shorts and trainers all the while hoping the man upstairs hadn’t heard anything. Tears ran down my face, slow and with purpose. Thoughts and feelings were building inside of me. I had to run to get away. Closing my front door behind me, I ran to the forest behind my parent’s home. My feet fell, one in front of the other, each fall sounding out like the beat of a drum. It was chanting things that I didn't want to hear. They chanted about life and death and fairness and unfairness. On the soft forest floor, they were muffled and I was relieved. I ran on and on into the wood that had been a sanctuary for me in my late teen years and early twenties – the time when my parents moved out of Hackney and into the suburbs. It was where I had gone to dance and to talk to the Goddess. I had done healing there and manifested there. As I weaved through the great Oaks, I was sixteen again and looking for comfort but I couldn't stop. Memories were chasing me. I was almost at my favorite place now. A great clearing where there was just a green grass carpet and a sky ceiling. Flowers grew in clusters on the outskirts and little sandy hills had formed that were great for sitting on and reflecting. Everything was so vibrant in September. But as I ran to the end of the path I knew would lead me into the clearing, I stopped in shock at the sight before me. All of the green grass had gone. Everything living there had been taken up and the land had been flattened into dead, yellow straw-like Earth. I simply could not believe my eyes. I had walked there, only two days prior. Now, it resembled a barren wasteland and in the corner, a family had planted a tree in memory of their son who had killed himself. In all of the fifteen years I had been coming to this section of forest, I had never seen anything planted there in someone's memory. It was as though I was confronting Death. It had me by the horns and wasn't going to let go until I learnt what it had to teach me. So I threw my head back and dropped to my knees to show Death I would surrender.

There was no one moment of illumination where I conceived the notion to go back to Syria. It was merely 'there', resounding within me, like destiny. I didn't try to deny it, but instead explored it over the days that followed. It felt like God's will. Like surrender; like all trace of 'me' had disappeared and there was only God left; like I had reverted back to infant-hood – loving, trusting and resigned to my parent. It was like he had scooped me up in his wide-open arms and asked me to disregard everything I thought I knew about life, death and love. I watched it happen within me, as if I were an outside observer. The meditations were flooding in and out like the tide – coming and going – as consistent as they were reliable:

I must give my love to Saleh.

I must show him I love him.

I must love him in a holy way.

I want to learn to love like God.

I can see his spirit.

I just need to love.

Where there should have been devastation raging inside me, there was peace and where there should have been despondency, there was love and I was accepting and compliant. Although the change in me was sudden, it wasn't a violent, fiery possession that overtook me and left me limp and docile to its will. It was a choice I made, provoked by the death of Hassan and strengthened by my feelings for Saleh. At some point, after learning that Hassan had been killed, I must have *agreed* to live a life guided by love because these inexplicable emotions were so real to me and I held no regard – whether stupidly or not – for the consequences I would suffer – physically or emotionally.

I had believed that I was confronting Hassan's death in the forest the day I heard the news of his passing, when in fact I assume now that I was confronting my own. That was the day I died to the 'Tina' I thought I knew and was reborn into someone who wanted to understand God – to emulate him – to see humanity through his eyes and ultimately, I ended up handing over my trauma to him. I wanted to become that empty vessel so often talked about – a person that conforms to God's will and knows when to cling tight and when to let go. And so I can say, that the ramification in consigning my love and entrusting God with my soul, was the forging of a close bond between he and I for he was now my Lord and I, his handmaid.

Chapter 30

"I've sold my gold jewelry."

"What? What do you mean? Why?" Rumi sounded scared but she knew me very well because we had been friends since school. She knew what I was like. My levels of spontaneity these past couple of years had even surpassed her own as an experimental teen in nineties London. When she had heard that Hassan had been killed, she should have known that there would be a reaction.

"I've sold it and I've just come out of the Syrian embassy. I had to apply for a visa. I am going to Damascus."

"But there's a war starting. There are bombs going off Tina. Where are you?" I envisioned her almond eyes widening and knew she would probably be twirling her thick black locks around her forefinger: one of her nervous habits.

"In Hyde Park." I didn't know where I was going but I knew I had to keep walking to burn off the adrenalin pumping through my body – a sensation that would remain with me until I boarded the plane at Heathrow.

"I just gave them my passport. They will send it back with the visa in the post, if they give it to me that is. They can still say no. If they do, I have a friend in Amman in Jordan. I have a plan to get across the border and….." Rumi interrupted the flow of disturbing information to shout,

"What!" a few more times in shock and then went silent. I would still end up going anyway. She knew what I was like. My mind had been made up.

"I am only going to tell you." I said, determination in my voice "and if anything happens to me, you must tell my family."

It was a great burden to put on my friend's shoulders but I knew my friend had a thirst for adventure too. She had responsibilities at home, coming from a traditional Indian family and had never been able to travel as much as she would have liked. I hoped that she would want to be in it with me.

A few days later, I got my passport through the letterbox with a visa stuck proudly on one of the few remaining empty pages. I grasped at it in delight. I had arranged everything. I would land in Damascus and my friend Faruk would pick me up. He would take me to Sara's family home where I would stay and what would happen next I didn't know. I would surprise Saleh when I got there. At that point, all I wanted to do was pay my respects to his family and let him know I cared for him. I was just saying I loved him without actually speaking the words. What could be so bad about that? Rumi warned me that he might feel I was trapping him but I was on a mission and be it right or wrong, I couldn't stop myself from going through with it. I was fulfilling a mission in God's name. A very simple mission that wouldn't land me in the local paper or win me an award, but it would show a young man who had lost hope in the world, God's love for him; the simple act of being there for someone when they need you. Everyone does it. But this time it involved me travelling into a developing civil war.

People in wars need love too, I wrote to Sara as we arranged plans for my arrival. I knew what Saleh was like and that he would not react like a character from a black and white movie that would sweep me up in his arms and kiss me passionately and declare his undying love. I knew he would push me away but I was compelled to confront my feelings for this man. It was almost like I wanted to test myself – would I be able to love in the same way God loves us? He sees us and he knows our souls. I felt I could see Saleh – deep into his spirit – and all the times I interpreted as him being mean, were brushed to the side and replaced with a vision of a perfect soul who needed support.

Just as I had experienced with Ryan, I had fleeting moments when I realized that I wasn't *forgiving* him – I was acknowledging that there was nothing to *forgive* and that every time I contributed to the notion of forgiveness, I was implying that Saleh had done something against me to begin with. Which may be true in this split second in a soul's existence we call life, but in the grand scheme of things – in the eternity that is our spirit – in the perfection that is our soul – in the connection to God we have – I recognized that I was harming no one but myself. I had an overwhelming awareness that I was severing my own divine connection to God, and all to hold onto negative beliefs about my fellow brother. I was ready to release all of my previously held notions about what love was and what people were about. I wanted to experience a different form of love and I decided this would be my attempt to love in a holy way.

Extract from my personal diary:

A man I barely know said something to me last night after listening to my story. It was 'The reality of nature and the beauty of the world teaches us that only that is truth.' Nothing exists except love. Maybe it would be more fitting to address God as 'Love' because then all the beliefs of the ego cannot be conjured up at the mere mention of His name.

My beloved Hassan has been immortalized in love. He's gone and my heart is aching with love that only love can repair. I feel your death, Hassan, has pushed me to a new level in the few days since it happened so I will keep this diary over this period of time to record my trip to Syria and to demonstrate how even the pain of losing someone cannot lay its black cloak over love's flourishing beauty.

By now I had been in contact with Syrian friends for updates, letting them know that I was coming back and most of them talked about small protests and enormous rallies. There were occasional shootouts and soldiers forming checkpoints around the city but the worst events were taking place in Hama and Homs. I wasn't anticipating too much trouble in the capital and planes were still flying there so it couldn't be that bad, I had told myself to calm my nerves. But they weren't centered round the possibility of war. They would peak when I thought of being able to say goodbye to Hassan and also when I thought about Saleh, having to live his life in this country where young men specifically were being targeted by the authorities. What if he were killed too?

I would actually be giving myself a chance to close a chapter in my life. Not many people have the courage to face their perceived source of pain. I wanted to be able to say I had done that and inspire others to do it too. Who knew? Maybe one day I would have children to encourage and grandchildren to entertain. Maybe I would be able to tell them stories of true love and love for friends in foreign, exotic lands. So I took a pen and began to write a letter to God but the first words read '*Dear Love*' and my hand just kept moving until I had released my emotions.

Dear Love,

This is a letter to Saleh.

I haven't seen you for many months but I know you are the one for me. If not romantically from your side, I will be happy to show my love for you. I have a desire to show you that you are loved. You are beautiful to me. You lost your mother and your brother but I want you to feel their love for you, through me.

The love that will take you to Heaven on Earth is the one where you receive back what you didn't expect. I am prepared for anything. At least I would have shown my love for you: my devotion to healing your heart and healing my own.

I didn't read it back, but lit a white candle on my wooden bedside table. I closed my eyes and breathed deeply. My stomach was in knots but I let my hands guide me as I began to write again.

It feels right at this time in my life to replace God's name with 'Love'.

When I finally read the words aloud in the candlelight, I was dumbfounded. I was renaming God. But I was filled with so much love that it felt right. *A Course in Miracles* says nothing is real except love and so my spiritual journey was never a case of trading in the divine feminine for the divine masculine. It has always been about the war between what is real (anything that unites us together) and what is illusion (anything that separates us from each other).

It was real love that had brought me together with Hassan and it was with real love that people were crying for him all over the world. How people think we are anything other than love was beyond me at that moment in time. I saw with clarity that although Hassan was physically gone, he had left love behind. Trails of love following him like a plane doing acrobats in the sky. Yes. *Love* would be God's new name. Genderless, selfless, Love.

Chapter 31

Eight days after Hassan was killed, I was boarding a plane to Damascus, via Dubai. With me I had one suitcase, my notebook, which doubled up as a diary, money from selling my jewelry because I hadn’t worked all summer and a return ticket for ten days time. I loved that notebook. Its pages were bordered with glittered roses and cherubs. It had belonged to my nan.

A Course in Miracles was at home lying peacefully on my bookshelf. I had read it intermittently several times and done some of the lessons in the workbook for students, but I wouldn't have time to focus on it for the next couple of weeks so I decided to leave it behind. Anyway, I trusted that I was experiencing a form of direct communication with *Love* that I didn't require the book to complete. Looking at my little notebook, I figured I could try to write my own course in miracles. What I was about to do would no doubt teach me more about life than any book could so I took a picture of Jesus with me instead. It also belonged to my nan and was him, sitting on a log amongst nature. Whenever I was afraid I could hold him and remember that he was around to guide me as a brother looking out for his little sister.

There were Syrians and other Arabs aboard the plane. I was the only 'foreigner'. I didn't think I had ever lived so much in the moment in my entire life. Whenever I felt nauseous with apprehension, I would remind myself of where I was. *I am sitting in an economy seat on Emirates. I am sitting in an economy seat on Emirates. I am sitting in an economy seat on Emirates.* I took out my notebook and wrote down my fears of being arrested or refused entry into Syria at the airport. At such a tense time, it was obvious that security would be more alert than usual. My friends had heard rumors that security was checking *Facebook* profiles before people left and entered the country! No doubt hunting for people who were not supporting the president. I was not stupid enough to comment on the politics either way because I didn't want to offend my friends. I just hoped they would have records showing my profession as a teacher because if they suspected me of being a journalist, I would have no chance of getting in.

Diary extract:

I am on the plane to Dubai right now. I'm so afraid. I'm so in despair. I'm so resigned. At moments like these there's nothing left to do but give yourself to Love completely and fully. Anything that happens to me now is in the hands of Love. Everything I have done in my life, I've done because I want love.

At Dubai airport I slept fitfully in one of those chairs cruelly crafted from cold metal, into a bed as if to lure you into a false illusion of comfort. I also took a few minutes to write. It was a release.

Please love. Fill Saleh's heart with your energy. Let him forgive my mistakes. Let him see the light and know that fear and our Earthly selves are not capable of blocking love.

My writings read more like a series of prayers yet I continued:

Love exists to give us a divine purpose, greater than ourselves. We must force ourselves to grow in order to match it. Saleh is the man I want to marry but our destiny I hand over to Love whose main aim is to make me happy.

I was startled at my penned admission of romantic love for Saleh. Of course I was sad that we had not worked out because I put so much energy into our relationship but after everything I had gone through when I lived in Damascus the first time around, the fact that I was not seen as marriage material for him by his father, should have been a deal breaker. A marriage between us was tantamount to impossibility. Yet I continued to write, a scribe for a voice I wanted to give credence to.

I have no expectations though because this is such a strange situation – I am travelling to an unstable country. I've lied to get here. Sold and spent to gain the funds I need, begged help from people that I do not really want to approach. I may also have lost my private students back in London and my only form of income right now. Here I am about to enter a place where they may arrest me and I am putting my physical self in danger. Maybe I will have to die on this trip because I am finally chasing love. I am doing this as a spiritual journey because I want to acknowledge the presence of love and I do deserve to be happy. My darling Hassan; there are no words. My love. My brother. You are affecting everyone and everything with the tides of the love you have left behind.

Four hours later I made the ten-minute walk over to my gate, took another disagreeable seat and noticed I felt really sick. Unhealthy food, dehydration and tiredness do not mix well together. Mental pictures of being arrested and locked away in a Syrian dungeon came and went and tears filled my eyes as I thought of how I had told my entire family and friends I was on my way to France. Only Rumi knew where I was going. I closed my eyes in a dramatic display of 'what have I done?' and opened them again to find a face about a ruler's length from my own. Frizzy, sun-kissed hair, white teeth and a freckled face were all I saw.

"Hey mate! Ya not Syrian then?" I needed a second to gain my composure. I saw it was a woman with a young son. She was older and Australian. Definitely Australian."I thought I was the only one! I'm so glad you're here too!" she chirped. She laughed; like an alarm clock, but a good one because it woke me up out of my tired stupor and brought me back to reality. All thoughts of dungeons and torture disappeared and now I had made a friend. "My husband is Palestinian. He lives in Damascus, in Meze! D'ya know it? This is our son Georgie. Say hello Georgie." He was a handsome little boy, confident and articulate and he greeted me politely.

"Err hi! Yeah I know Meze. My name is Tina by the way, what's yours?" The gate opened and we both stood up and grabbed our bags. The woman was attractive with long hair, a thin frame and she was wearing a hippie chic long dress, with matching purple lens sunglasses perched on top of her head. She made me feel scruffy in my jeans and sweater but she was a Godsend. She was the perfect person to disperse my nerves because I couldn't help but retain a bemused look on my face for the next five hours.

"I'm Poppy. Originally from New Zealand but now living in Australia. That's where I met my husband."

"Ah so you have never been to Syria before?" She looked at me with happy eyes and said,

"No. I can't believe we are moving there can you Georgie?" Georgie gave his mum a high five and an excitable "yeahhhh".

Wow. This family has energy I thought after Poppy explained she had been travelling for twenty hours already. As she went to take her seat, she said she would see me on the other side and I said something along the lines of,

"Aren't you worried about moving your son to Damascus? What with the situation and all? The protests, the bombs, the shootings?" Poppy leant over and in an *attempt* to whisper, because she obviously couldn't control her energy levels, said,

"Whaddya mean protests?"

I needn't have worried about going through security at Damascus airport. As I stood in line, a white American man was ahead of me and I watched in horror as the guard asked him why he wanted to enter Syria, listened to his claim that it was 'tourism' related and saw him get whisked off to a private room for questioning. When it was my turn I was not asked for the reason behind my stay, nor anything related to my career. He waved me through as though he had seen my face a thousand times and had become bored of it. He barely acknowledged my existence. And then it came to me. How could I have forgotten? Silly Tina. All that drama for nothing: he had seen my breasts through the façade! I was a *woman*. I lacked brawn and muscles and I didn't know what else made me different from a man in this world except for the obvious, but it was no doubt as shallow as that. The guard had therefore deemed me unable to spy on a country, unable to hold down the profession of journalist, unable to protest against a regime. I was no threat to them but I wasn't sure if I should be pleased or offended. *Welcome to Syria*. I was definitely *back*.

Chapter 32

Faruk picked me up at the airport and drove me to Sara's house. Everything looked the same. The roads were the same. There were the picnicking families by the side of the highway. There was the old city. It had more police hanging around it but other than that, there was nothing immediately concerning. Faruk asked me about my friend's death and he told me about trouble he was having with his girlfriend. He was an old student of mine; a very respectful young man who went out of his way to help others. I was so grateful to him for being that friendly face when I had been so agitated at the airport.

I was also excited to see my old friends again and they were very welcoming. Sara's parents ushered me through the front door and her mum made me tea. Exhaustion weighed heavily on my eyes but I still had some adrenalin pumping through my body and I wasn't ready to sleep yet. In all, my journey had taken about twenty hours. I told Sara about the funny lady at the airport and we looked at each other in disbelief that she had not known about the situation in Syria. Poppy had approached me numerous times during the flight and had shouted out various red flag words such as *"War?" "Bombs?"* and *"President Assad?"* causing me to hide my face in embarrassment and sometimes fear. I wondered if this woman had been living under a rock for the past six months. I knew that people from down-under were laid back but come on! Sara commented on not liking the sound of Poppy's husband, who would instigate a move to a country on the brink of war, bringing his six-year old son and his naïve wife and that his family was probably in support of the regime. Regime supporters were famously known for being 'in denial' about the severity of the situation at that time. I nodded my head in agreement. So far everything was how it used to be for me except for the fact that I didn't have my flat to go home to after dinner. Sara's mother looked more stressed than usual. Her hair was thinner and her frame reflected that of a fragile china doll. I wanted to hug her and say everything would be okay but I didn't know if it would be. Syria was delicate and its people were delicate. They had so much to lose. Not only physical things but ways of life that had developed as well. They didn't want to turn into a hostile, angry country like certain other places in the Middle East. Syrians had worked so hard to maintain their society and independence. Now, Sara's family was talking of heading to their homeland. After lots of tears, laughs and general catching up, we headed to bed. Excitement kept me awake as I lay under the moonlight beaming in through the balcony windows. I had achieved my goal of getting there but I hadn't actually planned what to do next.

The next day was a fresh start. I had showered and put on clean clothes and spent the day with Sara, talking and having lunch in Qassar, the Christian quarter where she lived. This was probably my favorite place in Damascus. I always made Sara take me around there at Christmas time. It was beautiful, as every house was decorated with colorful lights and giant snowmen and Christmas trees. It could be gaudy at times, but I didn't care. It was similar to home. I was in awe and respect of the Muslim families who also wanted to join in the festivities. It was quite normal to see trees in their windows too and commonplace for them to take food to their Christian neighbors during the season, as a gift. Syria really was a uniquely spiritual place and when I could get past the stressors of being a single female Westerner living there, my heart would swell with pride at the fact that I had been witness to so much beauty in a very misunderstood people.

"So, when are you going to let Saleh know you are here?" Sara asked as she watched me squash my mashed potato and cheese down with my fork. "And aren't you going to eat that?"

"I feel sick. I mean it. I feel physically sick with the thought of surprising Saleh. I don't know why. What's the worst that can happen? He refuses to see me and you and I spend a happy holiday together?"

"Yes and that sounds good. But you *are* going to tell him and he is *not* going to be angry. Worried you are here, yes. Angry? No way. He knows he has to marry you." I almost choked on my tea.

"What do you mean Sara? I told you, I'm not going down that road again." She was clouding my brain and it was starting to irritate me. She knew I had messed things up with him and she knew I was there for Hassan. I felt my eyes well up with tears with the thought of him. I presumed what I had written in my diary about wanting to marry Saleh was just wishful thinking and getting caught up in the moment but she could see it too?

"He knows very well Sophie, that if he doesn't marry you, he will regret it for the rest of his life." She looked so certain I wondered if she had been asking about him on her weekly visits to the 'psychic' lady. I could calm my mind and logically reassure myself that what she had said wasn't true, but I couldn't control the fluttering of my heart.

I managed to put off the inevitable until the evening. I had to call Saleh and tell him I wanted to pay my respects to his family but it terrified me. Going through airport security would be nothing compared to this. I had so many worries. What if he felt trapped? What if I was putting him and his family in danger by contacting him? Their son had been killed in an emerging conflict and now they were talking with a British person. What if the police thought I was a journalist and then came to arrest me, and his family? They were definitely legitimate concerns, but overriding them was the knowledge that the government at this point in time, didn't want the world to be aware that there was an issue. They kept secret, the protests that happened, dispersing them quickly. They censored the news and social media sites were constantly brought down so that locals could not get information out regarding what was happening in their area. They granted me a visa for entry because they did not want anyone to think there was a problem. Doing so would shake faith in the president. This was a theme that I had noticed before the unrest. One day, during my initial stay in Syria, I had been walking back from work when two men attacked me suddenly on a side road. They attempted to restrain me and put me into their car, but I managed to get away with the help of some customers at a nearby café. The British school called the police and the chief questioned me. When we were done, he said nothing revealing about procedures or consequences that would take place, instead he looked me square in the eyes and broadcast his prepared speech.

"Syria is very safe, this is not a usual occurrence. Syria is the safest country in the world". It was as though someone had inserted a computerized command into his brain and I ended up feeling his one goal in dealing with me was to promote Syria as 'safe' for Westerners. From Sara's cozy bedroom, I knew that the last thing they would want to do is arrest me for the attention it would bring and so they would merely sit in the shadows and watch.

Sara got up to leave the room and gave me a look of encouragement. My phone was sitting on the dressing table and so I picked it up slowly all the while feeling my stomach clench up. I dialed his number. It rang for a while and then,

"Aloo?"

"Err hi Saleh."

"Ahlan! Ahlan! Welcome. That you?"

"Yes it's me." A pause.

"The number. It looks strange you know?"

"Yes. I'm here. I'm in Damascus."

"What are you doing here? It's really dangerous. You know, we have a serious situation here right now."

"I just had to see you."

"I can't believe it! I can't believe."

"I'm sorry but I had to."

"Ok, Ok are you with Sara?"

"Yes"

"I am coming there. Wait for me."

Sitting in the car, he would steal glances at me as he drove, with a mixture of concern and annoyance. But the reason our relationship had always been so volatile was because he knew he could never hold me down. I was spontaneous and independent and it fascinated him and disgusted him at the same time. I couldn't speak Arabic and he couldn't speak fluent English and so we had always had to communicate in a very simple way. As a result, we found simplicity in each other when actually we were both very complex people.

"I can't believe you are here. This is crazy. I didn't think I would see you again." He said. He put his hand out to touch me as he steered, like a blind man feeling for familiarity.

"I know it's a difficult time for you and your family, but if I could just pay my respects, I will not bother you again."

"What do you mean, bother me?" his face looked paler than usual and washed out under the orange glow of the street lamps, his eyes like black holes.

"Well, our last conversation, you said you didn't want to see me again. You don't have to you know… but please let me say goodbye to Hassan."

He nodded his head but didn't give much away. I tried to intuitively discern what was going through his mind and knew that night that a part of him was dead over the loss of his brother and that it made him more conscious of the loss of his mother. A loss he never really had the chance to confront because he had been a teenager at the time and he hadn't known how. There was a hollow-ness to him that wasn't there before. The only way I could explain it to Sara afterwards was that there were shadows in his eyes. I understood that he felt very alone but I was not naïve enough to presume that me being there would heal that.

We drove around the city and he shouted for revolution. He told me that he was attending a protest coming up. I could almost hear the whirring from his brain and the exhaustion of thought had paled his face and created furrows in his brow. I felt afraid for him but had no response because I wasn't in his position and had no idea what it was like to lose my sister at the hands of the government. I suspected I would be calling for revenge too.

As usual, there were no false declarations of love or even any tears shed when I saw him for the first time in nine months. I trod carefully and listened to him. He was so strong and competent but I couldn't help see him as a delicate newborn that needed looking after and it was a bizarre sensation for me. I couldn't explain it but I felt protective over Saleh. As we passed checkpoints in the road with armed soldiers, I knew for sure that had they fucked with him, I would have taken the bullet instead. Primal woman was tearing at my insides, writhing to be unleashed as I looked into the faces of those young soldiers. If they had fucked with my love, I would have torn their eyes from their sockets. That's how I felt for Saleh at that moment. And it definitely shocked me however, I could do nothing but go with the flow and respect the martyr side of myself: the *Kali* within me, and the mother Goddess that stirred in my soul. It was obvious he was living in another time. We were in his dad's car, but he was outside the gates of the presidential palace, screaming about the unjustness of it all. We were holding hands but he wasn't with me. So I left him that night and watched him drive away with concern etched over my face. Primal woman was still twisting and turning and she was whispering, *"not fair. Why him?"*

Saleh had said he would be in contact within the week so that we could organize a time for me to see his family. All I wanted to do was be there with them, say I was sorry for their loss and try not to make it too personal and about me. Whatever part of me this involved, it would be an internal healing that was between *Love* and I and that also contributed to the reasons why I had lied to everyone back home about where I was going. I didn't want opinions, or horrified looks or even interest. Hassan's death had instigated a spiritual journey and I hoped that wherever spirit was leading me, that I would take from it what was needed. In the meantime, four days after I arrived in Damascus, Saleh found a room for me to rent in an old Arabic house in Sarooja: a very central part of the city that was near to the main government building. I had thanked Sara's family and given them gifts of appreciation for allowing me to stay there whilst I found somewhere to rent. I still had over a week before my flight back to England.

He drove me to the new house, my one suitcase in his hand and led me up to the gate. As usual, these old houses had only a steel door fixed into an enormous wall, with no windows providing clues as to what resided within. A skinny, tanned young man with jet-black hair shaved close to his head answered. He seemed extremely friendly as he began talking with Saleh in Arabic. He had a nice energy and I liked him immediately. Leading us inside, I looked around. The house was okay. My room was horrible; so cold and bare. But it had an en-suite shower room and the mattress was clean and that was the most important thing. The walls were white but held no warmth in that particular shade. The house was very old and it showed. I didn't mind that much though. It was clean and had what I needed considering I had brought nothing with me. At the back of my mind, I wondered why Saleh would choose this place for me. It wasn't cheap. Rents had gone way up since war had stirred in Hama and Homs. People wanted to move out of the smaller cities and into Damascus where it was safer and the landlords were profiting off of the boom. So why did he want me to live in this place where I was the only girl and where my room resembled a high security prison cell? I learnt that night there were four men living in the house who had moved out of their areas that had been taken over by military. They were students in their early twenties. The man who had opened the door was called Ahmad. He had also fled his Kurdish village for the safety of the capital so that he could continue studying philosophy at university.

As I settled down for the evening, I heard Saleh leave and I knew that he was asserting his authority over me again. I couldn't understand why he did that if he didn't want to be in a relationship with me. The school I had worked for had closed down and I was there alone. The British embassy had been trying to contact me for the past few days, warning me of the dangers of remaining in the country but I had just ignored them. I was completely alone and one of a very small number of foreigners who were in Syria at that time, and who were not there because they were married or engaged to a Syrian. Saleh had given me some money before he left, and I knew that things would either get a lot worse between us or a lot better. For the first time, I was dependent on him.

The next day I had a meeting with my old manager at the school who was in the process of finalizing things before they closed the offices completely. I wanted to enquire about a paycheck I was owed. I got dressed in a pair of black trousers and a T-shirt and slipped on some ballet flats. I despised the 'I'm a tourist' look where women would put on a massive scarf and open toed sandals. My best bet for living there alone was to blend in. I had always worn 'normal' clothes before, even skirts above the knee. I brushed my hair. I had blonde highlights put in a year before and somehow they had expanded to cover most of my head. I wasn't sure I liked being blonde in this country where it made a woman stand out immensely so I considered popping into my regular hairdresser and getting a brown dye put on it. As I opened the door to my room, I saw Ahmad sweeping the floor. He had a red bucket of water next to him filled with bleach. It smelled so fresh after a night in my dusty room. I still had a couple of hours before my meeting so I proceeded to open my window and air out my space. Ahmad threw the bucket of water onto the floor and started to mop. He looked at me curiously.

"How are you? I didn't get to speak properly to you last night. You are very quiet". He grinned at me, his eyes wrinkling at the corners. I had been sizing him up and deemed him harmless. I was very careful about the men I spoke to, always trying to determine their intentions, especially after the Egyptian incident. But this man seemed to have no agenda. He was well spoken with excellent English. He was only young but he had been aged by a life of poverty and hard work. As he cleaned I was comfortable enough to sit down and watch him. And that was when I experienced the sense of freedom. I was away from England in this place where it was so warm my feet were sweating in my shoes. The sun beat down on us as we moved through this house with no roof. Blue and white tiles decorated the floor and red and white tiles lined the walls. It was very traditional. Jasmine flowers were in full bloom in their pots that Ahmad had tended to. Watching him do something so simple, in such a beautiful setting made me feel joyful. As he worked he told me about himself. He was careful not to stare at me for too long. Maybe he didn't want me to feel uncomfortable around him or maybe he was shy. I noticed the strength in his arms and legs despite his thin frame.

"I have many British friends. And American and Australian. You are from London?"

"Yes I am."

"I had a British girlfriend once!" He bent down to scrub a particularly grubby tile and smiled up at me. I understood that he was very proud of his work, so I raised my eyebrows to show that I was impressed.

"Oh yeah?"

"Yes. She was forty three years old." I laughed at the revelation. "Yes, I am younger. I am twenty-one." I recalled once seeing a Syrian, the same age, with a Western woman who must have been in her fifties.

"I didn't know Arabs are into sugar-mummies! I thought that was a Turkish thing. I'm half Turkish."

"Yes your boyfriend told me last night." I laughed again in surprise but wouldn't allow myself to feel the tingle of hope that he may have told this man I was his girlfriend.

"Believe me, he is not my boyfriend." Ahmad didn't look as though he believed me.

"I lived with my British girl for a year but then we broke up. I didn't work and I think she wanted me to." Satisfied that he had cleaned the tile, he set to work watering the Jasmine plants. Their sweet, elegant fragrance wafted by me as the pressure of the cascading water shook the buds, sending their petals floating to the floor. I went over and scooped them in my hands, rubbing them between my palms to transfer their scent onto me. *Beautiful*, I thought, as I breathed it in. I discerned that he was watching me out of the corner of his eye. My face flushed. "I also had an American girlfriend. She was older too. Actually I am going to a party tonight with a German friend," Ahmad continued, observing my embarrassment with a grin. I gathered that he wanted to manipulate my view of him. Just because he was a village boy it didn't mean he was closed minded and ignorant of other cultures but he needn't have bothered because I found him a breath of fresh air. As we conversed, I learnt he was a philosopher. He spouted verses from the poetry of *Gibran* and *Rumi* and yet he was innocent, filled with contemplations on the true nature of romance and God.

We spoke until it was time for me to leave. He offered to walk me to the school but I said I would like to go alone. I hadn't had any time to myself since I had got there and I wanted a walk. As I got onto the bustling streets I wished I had accepted his offer and I cursed Saleh and his ego. This was a horrible part of town. I hadn't passed that way much when I had lived in Damascus previously. There wasn't anything much around there for Brits to do. Now I couldn't believe it. People were constantly staring at me and making comments. I distinctly heard "Russian" several times from different men. I assumed my hair made me look as though I were Russian so I just frowned and kept walking. As I got into the part of town where the school was, I sighed in relief. It was a busy shopping center with normal people who barely bat an eyelid at me. Many had seen me from the two years before and knowing I was British, were surprised that I had returned. I could see it in their faces. My manager was also astonished that I was back considering I had broken my contract three weeks early but I lied and said I was engaged because I didn't want everyone to know about my involvement with someone who had been killed by the regime. It was too risky. My old manager paid me there and then and I was really grateful. The first thing I did was book an appointment at the salon to have my hair dyed back to my natural brown.

Chapter 33

Every time I would leave that house for the next week, I would have to ask Ahmad what a new word meant. I realized I had been lazy the first time I had lived in Syria and had barely a clue about the Arabic language. This time though, I had been forced to listen and learn. However, I wasn't expecting to learn that 'Russian' in Syria, was synonymous with the word 'prostitute'. I had seen the Russian girls walking through Sarooja, where I lived, and they looked completely out of place on a Middle Eastern street. They had a fierce-ness about them as they strutted around in stripper heels and little tops. They were advertising to the world that they were prostitutes. The truth was that Syrian men ran brothels and it would have been illegal to use local women for them and so they used Russians instead. I didn't know the story behind them but figured that many had either been tricked or sex-trafficked into the country. It made me feel sick because I had heard that Saleh and his friends might use Russian prostitutes as did a lot of the wealthy young men in Syria but I was too afraid to ask him in case he said yes. I would rather not know.

Ahmad was outraged when I asked him what it meant and discovered that men had been shouting it at me as I walked down the road. He was even angrier when I innocently asked what '*sharmouta*' meant. His face screwed up in disgust he stood up from the sofa abruptly and threw down a piece of bread he was about to break.

"Who the fuck called you that? Fucking idiots!" he shouted. "Was it the man in the shop across the road? He's a fucking idiot!"

"No. I don't know who they are but mainly it's the bastards in the shops along the main road."

"It means slut but it is worse than that in Arabic. It is a very bad word." In my first two years in Syria I had learnt some pretty ridiculous things could indicate a woman of 'low morals,' for instance, if she was out walking a dog or if her hair was wet. Both could mean that the woman was a prostitute. I looked back at him, my mouth open and put my face in my hands. I couldn't believe I was living there. There were so many better areas of Damascus, but this area was particularly known for foreign prostitutes. No wonder I was being called out as one. What horrible ignorant people they were. I wasn't bothering anyone or wearing anything inappropriate. I couldn't relate to people who would be so disrespectful. "Next time you go out, I'm going to walk behind you. Allah help anyone who says anything and I hear!"

He sat down and started eating again, shaking his head as though he were in some inner dialogue with himself. It made me feel awful. All I had to do was exist and as a result, viewed as some kind of whore, worthy only to be looked down upon as a bane to society. I excused myself and went to shower. A couple of days later I had my hair dyed. The comments were still there but reduced somewhat although I wondered if it was just wishful thinking. I absolutely hated living in that area but it had always been popular with foreigners so I couldn't understand why these men were acting like villagers. In the hot September sun I made sure I always wore trousers and long sleeves with flat shoes. My mantra was to look as boring as possible.

Chapter 34

Saleh had been in touch and he was taking me to see his family at their villa. It would be a relaxed affair so I wasn't feeling too nervous about it. I hadn't heard too much from him over the week or so that had passed but I was distracted with making new friends and meeting up with old ones. We would text or speak on the phone and I made sure he knew I was there if he needed to escape from his cold stepmother. Once he had confided that he felt ignored by her and that she didn't talk to him very often. It was one of the few fleeting moments that he had let me into his world and I treasured it. It broke my heart though. I didn't want him to feel alone and pushed out because he happened to remind the new wife of an old one.

Saleh's family were surprised to see me as I got out of the car and stood before them. They welcomed me and I did what I came for but quietly and discreetly. There were uncles and aunts and kids running around, so I just sat in on conversations, drank wine with his uncles and reminisced about Hassan with them. I didn't want to make a whole song and dance of it and behave dramatically. They were all in a state of shock but life had to continue and they had other young people in the family that it was their duty to protect. Most importantly, they were worried about their boys having to do military service. As Saleh was the only boy left on his biological mother's side, he did not have to do the service. If Hassan had been alive, both of them would have been called at some point. I listened to them discussing plans involving moving to Beirut for the time being. Saleh argued with his father and refused to go. The patio was quiet as he said he needed to stay and fight against the regime with the *Free Syrian Army*. His father just downed his whiskey and said nothing. *He really is a very unusual character*, I contemplated. He seemed so untraditional as though he didn't really belong in this country where you were encouraged to not think for yourself. He had an aura about him. He was the kind of person who could really make an impact and get people to listen to him. Saleh explained that after the death of Hassan, his father had actually had a meeting with government officials and requested permission to set up his own political party. I stared at Saleh in amazement.

"But that's impossible!" He just nodded his head and said,

"I know, I know. They said he wouldn't be allowed to do that of course." Everyone knew there was only one political party within the Syrian government. I was in awe of this man who responded to his soul and just did what his heart felt was right. Later his dad turned his attention to me.

“You are not a British spy are you?” I heard a few people laugh around me, so I assumed he was joking.

“No I’m not Doctor!” A serious glare through spectacles and pursed lips broke into an all out laugh. He was obviously pleased at his little joke and I wasn't sure if he had purposely tried to intimidate me. Saleh and I exchanged glances. I had broached the issue of his father hating me many times with him but he always denied it. The Doctor was a confusing man but I didn't mind being the butt of his jokes if it meant he would smile. I had noticed how devastated he looked and I couldn't imagine the pain he must have gone through when he found out what had happened to his son. He had already lost his first wife and now another part of her that he could hold and talk to and experience, had left him behind. I couldn't comprehend the magnitude of the pain he must have been in.

As I left the villa that night, I knew that they were grateful I had come even though they did think I was mad for risking my safety to do so. The roads out of Damascus had changed and they were now lined with soldiers and checkpoints. As we passed, the car would fall quiet and my heart would beat a million miles an hour hoping they wouldn't flag us down. I was glad I had dyed my hair but luckily cars with women in, were not stopped as often as cars with men. This was advantageous for me because I knew if soldiers found a car with a foreigner inside at this awkward time in the country, when they suspected everyone of being journalists, it would have been their job to at the very least, to detain me at the side of the road and request more information from immigration or interrogate me and search me for clues as to what I was doing there. From the beginning my main aim was to avoid checkpoints at all costs. These were the cause of Hassan's death and they were run by jumped - up, ignorant, brainwashed, young men. They could not be relied upon for a logical determination of who I was and what my intentions were.

As Saleh drove down the highway, his cousins in the back, I wound down the window to catch blurred glimpses of the countryside. I had done it. I had paid my respects, I had trod on the grass where Hassan had existed and sat in the chair where he had laughed, and beside the fire where he had felt sadness. I hoped he was looking down from Heaven and felt glad that he had touched someone's life in such a way that they were willing to literally walk in his footsteps one last time. To breathe him in with the hope that remembering him would transfer some of his goodness, his strength and innocence into them. I was truly happy that night.

Now I had a decision to make. It was my last day in the country. Well my ticket said so anyway. I was in my room alone. I took out my notebook and decided to make a list of reasons to stay and reasons to go home. I came up with the following pros:

1. Money owed to me has come in at the exact right time!
2. I feel comfortable in Damascus and in no danger.
3. I am with Saleh.
4. I can help people
5. I love the lifestyle
6. I have emergency money in credit card to go home with

I read the list again. Strangely enough, *Love* had sent me a sign that I should stay in that money had inexplicably appeared in my account and I had no idea where it had come from. I frowned at number three. I didn't suppose that was a good enough reason because we were not in a relationship but I just loved to be in his presence. I also wasn't sure about number four but I was wiling to try. All the schools were closed but I was playing with the idea of private teaching for an English language exam that students needed, to be able to enter a British or American university. I had gone without money for long periods of time in London and private teaching might be the change I needed to be able to work hard and support myself.

I contemplated for a while longer and then began to write a list of cons.

They came slower than the pros and were short and sweet.

1. I can't tell my parents where I am
2. I can't access my UK bank accounts
3. I have no clothes with me
4. Saleh may not want me here
5. Unstable situation

I had called and told my parents that I was going to stay in Beirut with friends for a while. I loved my family – without them I would probably be lying dead in a gutter somewhere with only my *Course in Miracles* and a few bits of witchy paraphernalia to show for my life. We would hang out all the time, but nothing spiritually meaningful ever left their mouths. I was different from them all because I could feel that missing part of me – that void that Ryan and I had been searching to fill – calling and I just couldn't ignore it. My sisters were successful and spoke of their careers and their new cars and houses and I didn't even have a stable job. I wanted to talk of *Love* and the spirit. That would not have gone down well amongst such logical, practical people. To explain why I was in Syria, would have been speaking in a language they could never have understood and so I decided not to bother, as harsh as it seemed. When I made the call they hadn't seemed too concerned. They knew I was different now but they didn't know why. I just wasn't ready to go back because once I got on that plane I would never be able to return. I had too many *what ifs* floating around. What if Saleh really does love me and wants to be with me? What if something happens to Saleh and I am not around? What if I am here for these reasons and I am leaving too soon? It was these questions that prompted me to grab that airline ticket, scrunch it up and throw it in the bin. Eager to discover what else might be in store for me with the man I had to admit I was still very much in love with, and spurred on by the memory of Hassan, I had decided to stay.

Chapter 35

It was hard going at first. I couldn't access my money because the banks had no links to my accounts anymore. ATMs I had used in the past had now stopped working. I was also freezing because the weather had started to change and I had only packed summer clothes. When my money ran out, Ahmad and I would scrape our pennies together and he would go out and bring us food, whatever we could afford. We survived off of omelets and bread. Ahmad made the best omelets I had ever tasted in my life. He would add mint and sometimes he would add onion. It was so simple but I didn't know how he did it and I never managed to replicate the taste again. Maybe it was the taste of eating when you don't know where your next meal is going to come from. I knew I could have asked Saleh for money and he would have been obligated to give it to me - after all, I had lent him enough money in the past – but I didn't want to bother him too much what with everything he was going through.

Saleh and I had been out a few times and I sneaked him into my room once. My friend Poppy said I shouldn't have, but submitting to him was my way of showing I was a good person as I would put his needs before my own. I would take any opportunity to have his focused attention and to feel wanted and on the days I was sure he didn't love me even an ounce, I would sleep with him because I hoped he might in the future. On the days he appeared to love me behind the bravado, pressed up against him, I would imagine our hearts growing tentacles and merging together like interlocked fingers in a game of mercy. I'd give him what he wanted and he'd give me what I wanted so why did I feel as though I was the loser of a game? He'd sleep beside me but my bed seemed consumed by a vaster bleak emptiness, than when he wouldn't. I'd tell myself that sex was a way to claim someone and that our bodies coming together was an expression of the highest form of love but when he would tenderly rest his hand on mine or cradle me to his chest, I was a desolate house in a windswept field.

I didn't always notice these aftereffects of sex but when I did, I pushed them away in fear wondering if I had serious issues and concluding that I should see a doctor. How could I possibly feel this way when I had just slept with the man of my dreams, the man who owned me and gave me a reason to live and shunned other people to care for me? I recalled similar emotions at the beginning of my relationship with Ryan, but they had subsided. I couldn't remember when. However, Saleh and I had been together off and on for almost three years so I figured I should surely be comfortable with him by now. I couldn't understand it so I chose to ignore it and blame it, instead, on all the men who had frightened me and had tried to hurt me, so at night when I was alone in my room the pain of it would hit me like a tsunami and I would tumble onto my bed, clutching my chest, unable to breathe with sadness. The pain felt like guilt but I refused to acknowledge it. I was still fighting remnants of depression from my life in Syria the first time around on top of Hassan's death and I was concerned about Saleh's safety. I was resolute in my own mind about the pain being sadness. I wasn't ready to examine why I was experiencing guilt because a part of me knew that once I looked there, what I would find would be so overwhelming that I might not be able to cope.

However, it was clear that the loss of Hassan played a massive role in my rekindled depression and had profoundly effected me and I wasn't quite sure why. I had lost my beloved nan in February that year who was like a second mother to me and I barely shed a tear for her but not because I didn't care. It was because I knew she had lived a long and fulfilled life in stark contrast to this young man who hadn't even finished university. I had also lost one of my best friends to suicide in 2007. She jumped eight floors to her death from her Manhattan bathroom window. I remember I was sleeping when it happened – I felt as though I had literally been slammed 'back' into my body from above somehow. Whether I had left it I don't know but I woke with a jolt, knowing that someone had just passed away. I was so convinced, in fact, that I got up and wrote on a calendar hanging on my wall: *someone died tonight*. Her mother informed me of her suicide on that very date, a few weeks later and I was devastated at her loss but at peace because she was. If anything could prove to me that we are all one, it would be my experience of intuiting her passing.

I think the fact that Hassan's death was so unjust, bothered me the most. It also wasn't good that my relationship with Saleh was so wrapped up with the loss of Hassan. We were never strong enough *friends* to be able to get through it together. When I found out that Hassan was gone, there was a part of me that wanted to get to Damascus as soon as possible so that I could grieve with people who knew him. It took a while but I realized that Saleh didn't want to share that with me. I called him one evening, little over a fortnight into my arrival and he was out having fun with his friends. I heard them laughing in the background and smiled, hoping he was happy. That was soon wiped off of my face.

"What do you want? Why are you calling me?"

"I errr… just wanted to say hi and see how you are Saleh."

"Just leave me alone. Stop calling me!" He shouted. "Don't call my phone again. Leave me alone."

I hung up feeling ashamed and like a compete idiot. *If he doesn't want me here why is he sleeping with me? Why is he taking me out?* I felt my cheeks burn with embarrassment as I realized my presence there in Damascus was unwanted. I knew he was in pain but all the conviction I had possessed that my second journey to Syria had been a calling from *Love*, left me as I looked around at the cold desk, cold bed, cold wardrobe. *What have I done?* I despaired. *What am I doing here? He hates me like he never has before and all because I wanted to make sure he was okay.* I looked back at my notebook with all my ramblings about *Love* and ripped out some pages, throwing them across my room. With pent up anger and hurt from the past year rushing out of every pore, and every word from Jesus evaporating, I yelled,

"This is complete bullshit," internalizing Saleh's pain and making it feel like my own. "I must be losing it, to think that God is communicating with me…" I ran over to my bathroom mirror to look at myself and confirm my worthlessness. "Me? … Pathetic me? Living in this horrible old house at thirty years old, with nothing to show for my life? God doesn't speak to people like me." A lost face looked back at me. I didn't know her. I figured I had understood what she was looking for but staring into her eyes now, I truly didn't know anymore.

So I took a razor from my shower room and sliced it across my arms – a habit from childhood that I hadn't entertained since meeting Ryan. This was the first time I had felt the urge to do it. I looked at the shallow scratches – I never cut deeply because it's the tiny scratches that bring the most discomfort – and I cried with hatred for who I was. Why did I have to think everything was a sign from the Goddess or that I had an angel or that I could talk with God? *Why can't I just be normal like everybody else?* I was so angry. *A Course in Miracles* was supposed to have taken all the bad stuff away but I was still making mistakes. I noticed the scratches did nothing to diminish the pain of Saleh's words and rejection– *I need something stronger. These pills.* I reached over to my desk and worked up the courage to take them. I drank down six with some water and then three more. *Dare you to take more,* I thought, laughing out loud and I swallowed every tablet I had lying around my room. I needed to kill this worthless *freak* that doesn't know how to live amongst people and who does stupid things like gets on a plane to force love on a person in a war torn country. Then imaginings of home came to mind - not London, England, but our real home where our mother-father God awaits us. And so I took more pills. I wanted to go back home. I wanted to leave this disgusting body that makes mistakes and go to *Love*.

If *Love* was a person and had appeared to me then, I would imagine She would take a seat on the only chair in my lonely room – the one I use for my desk. I would rise from my cold bed and walk over to Her, teeth grinding together with the pain of abandonment and with one wave of my arm, sweep everything off of the table to show Her how angry with Her I was. Then I would bang my fists down until the skin split at the knuckles whilst screaming out all the promises She had made to me that She had broken. I would reel them off one by one and She would sit there and take it because She knew She had done me wrong. Where was the love She had vowed me? I was still single. Where was the acceptance? I was still an outsider. Where was the happiness? I was still dying inside.

I lay down on the floor, recounting every bad decision I had ever made and gave up the game to God. There was no pretending that I was the perfect person anymore. Now that Saleh had seen the truth of me, what was the point? Maybe this is what Ryan had seen in me too? I deserved all the pain I felt. Was it so bad that ancient Damascus had been my church and my cold little bare room in that cold house, my confessional booth? I could now go back to England after having tried my hand at this attempt to find a love that was holy. *I will book my ticket tomorrow. It's okay to fail.* I concluded, before passing out on the stone floor, dark red curtains swaying with the breeze escaping through cracks in the wall.

I remember waking up that night paralyzed. I could only move my eyes and the rest of my body was unresponsive, with no feeling, except a bizarre sensation in the palms of my hands. It was as though my very soul was being sucked out of them with a vacuum cleaner. So it was there that I focused, willing my soul not to leave me and trying to move again. I knew if I had just relaxed into it, I would have flown up, high above my physical self but I wouldn't allow it to happen. I was afraid to go when I had been offered the chance, but on waking, I was still most disappointed to find I had not died in my sleep: a feeling that haunted me many times over the coming months, making it evident that I was sliding into a very grey depression.

I felt physically fine throughout the next day, much to my dismay. Saleh's words echoed back to me and I wanted to punish myself for how stupid I had been to listen to my emotions in the first place. They weren't messages from God – they were the ramblings of a woman who had just lost a very good friend at the prime of his life and in a horrific way. We, as people, know that death is inevitable for the body, however we never look at a person we love and care about and envision them leaving this life with a bullet to the head. *It's shock*, I told myself, as I got ready to head out to my local Internet café to book a ticket home. *I'm just in shock.* Ahmad knocked on my door just as I had finished putting on my shoes and said he was about to make breakfast. He showed me a bag of pastries and pointed to a fresh pot of tea and I thought it was probably a good idea to eat first so as I waited for him to make some eggs I grabbed my notebook to explain to it why I was now leaving Damascus.

I stepped out of my room and into the open courtyard. There was a dried up fountain located right in the center of the living room; I was delighted to see that today Ahmad had fixed it to get it running water again. I put my hands under it and took in some deep breaths. *I tried to do what I thought was right. I must try not to be so hard on myself,* I pondered looking at my tired face reflected on the fresh water's surface. I settled on an ottoman cushion under the predictably blue sky, listened to a bird singing and picked up my pen to wait for a description of my current state to pour out onto the paper. I moved my pen hurriedly as was my habit when diary writing and I didn't realize what I had put down until I read it back. *I don't have Saleh to boost my confidence,* I wrote, *but I feel the best when I give him love, despite those things that frustrate my Earthly mind. I realize that Saleh is a massive challenge – he doesn't give me any compliments or sweet words yet I love him. Why? Because he is teaching me how to love. He is teaching me that love must resist all these pointless Earthly things. When I love Saleh I look beyond them.* I read this extract back several times because it rang so true to me. I had gone there to give someone love and I was leaving at the first sign of not getting something back in return? And that's when I was certain that I was on the right path and that I wanted to learn more about *Love*. I realized how far I had come and I wasn't about to turn back now. I needed to know where else this journey might take me – with or without Saleh - and I wanted it to be taken with the awareness that *Love* was by my side and in all that I do. I wasn't about to leave Syria yet.

Chapter 36

I was slowly gaining students by word of mouth, as many knew me from my time as a teacher at the most sought after school in the whole country. As I met new students they would show their surprise at me being there but I also noticed their fear and apprehension. Some, like Saleh's father, openly asked me if I was a British spy. I would react with laughter and although I knew they were trying to adopt a light-hearted manner, in Arabic, I knew they were commenting to their friends and family that I may have a hidden agenda. This country had changed so much in the few months I had been away from it. The question everyone would ask, in supermarkets, taxis and cafes was '*are you for or against the president?*' I couldn't believe my ears. If you were smart, prior to February 2011, you wouldn't even say the *word* '*president*' let alone ask if someone was for or against him. It was a brand new Syria. Everything seemed to be awakening and people were emerging from their shells like tortoises that had been asleep for a hundred years. They were speaking and asking questions and giving opinions. But I felt that they were asking the wrong questions. It seemed too simplified at times and perfect at others. It was such a complicated issue though, that I just tried to stay out of it as much as possible.

When potential students interrogated me about why I was in the country, I said it was for love and tried to appear as honest as I could to gain their trust. I had no hidden agenda; didn't care for politics and didn't pretend to know about it. Opinion was too divided for me to feel confident that I wouldn't offend anyone anyway. Despite what was happening in Hama and Homs, there were many people in Damascus who supported the regime wholeheartedly. I saw them at the rallies. My friends would drape themselves in the Syrian flag, paint their faces and march in the streets, chanting things I couldn't understand in more ways than one. They would conduct the rallies in the streets of Sarooja where I lived because it was so central and in close proximity to the presidential palace. I could hear it all from my living room but stayed home on those days in case there was any trouble. I knew people who were there willingly and I also knew people who were there against their will. A friend of mine had called me, angry, whispering that her manager had forced her to attend. If she didn't, colleagues could report her and she would probably be arrested at a later date or simply go missing. Just because a civil war was brewing, it didn't mean the military would take over the intimidation of the population. The secret police still held their firm position within society and anyone acting against the president would still be reported.

“Think about it.” Ahmad said, one morning as we heard the procession pass through the street outside. “If I hand someone over to the secret police for being against the president, I am showing that I support him and the police will leave me and my family alone.” Ahmad was firmly against the regime. A lot of Kurdish Syrians were but the government had brought in a system whereby they would be granted Syrian passports, as previously, they had not been recognized as being Syrian. It was a ploy to neutralize tensions and gain their support during the unrest. Ahmad wasn't impressed though and he and his friends, students at the university, were very much involved in protesting. One night he handed me a disc and asked me to keep it for him. He looked afraid and his hands were shaking but he looked me in the eyes and said,

“If anything happens to me, here is the number of the person to call. He will want the disc.” I didn't want to be caught up in anything political but I took it anyway and asked no questions. It was probably a lot safer with me than it was with him. I was at times, afraid for my male friends’ safety, especially Saleh’s. Since his outburst, he had texted a few times about mundane things as though that phone call had never happened but I was so busy with work I barely had time to think about him. I saw him a few times for food but I made sure my emotions were locked away – I was too afraid to be that vulnerable again. I cared but I couldn't let it show as I didn't want him to feel cornered and pressured and like he owed me something for being around. He didn't. All I wanted to do was be close to the people who had known Hassan as I thought it might help my healing at that point. In addition to Hassan's passing being traumatic, being in London felt so cold. He had never been there. We didn't share any memories there. Damascus was where our friendship had bloomed and all the places he took me to, I could go to them once more and sit where he sat and soak in his memory from the very places he took his breaths and spoke his words and looked upon. I decided to enjoy spending time remembering him in all the places we went to around the city.

Chapter 37

About a month into my time in Sarooja, I met up with an old student of mine. She was called Eva - twenty-two years old and wild. She was from a Christian family that lived just outside of the old city and they were the most fearless, inspirational people I met in the entire time I was there. Unlike a lot of Christians who felt they had to remain loyal to the regime; one, for their own safety and two, because the Assad's had granted them a peaceful country to live in, where they could freely practice their religion, this family were fiercely against the government.

The family consisted of two sisters in their twenties and an eighteen year old brother. Their parents were in their late forties but were not opposed to dressing in balaclavas and protesting on the streets of Damascus. They would often invite me round to drink vodka and they would put the television on, turn it up deafeningly loud, and flick onto channels that were playing chants, songs and reports that labeled Assad a murderer of the Syrian people. I felt nervous about it at first, but soon got swept up in the daringness of it all. If I was going to go, I wanted it to be like this: with people who had fought for what they believed in and were willing to die for it. They were not soldiers but they were fighting for the country they loved and I never failed to leave their house uninspired. This was what life was about: being spurred on by love. I could relate to that.

Eva called on a Thursday night and said we should go drinking so I got ready and she picked me up in her car at the bottom of my street. We went to a bar that I had been to with Hassan in the Christian quarter near to Sara's house. The music was loud and the décor was really modern. The bar was lit up with purple lighting and decorated with mirrors and rows of liquor bottles, ready to be drunk. I made sure we sat at Hassan's favorite place – by the bar. We made small talk until we started to get tipsy and dismissed the men bothering us for numbers. We just wanted to chat. At one point, Eva downed her wine and slammed her glass down on the table.

"I need sex!" she shouted. I burst into laughter.

"What? When? Why?"

"This fucking country" she slurred. "I can't have sex when I want to. But I need it! I need sex. Why do I have to be married? Why? Fucking Why?" I was astonished to hear this come out of an Arab girl's mouth, considering I had been torturing myself for the past few years, comparing myself to the virtuous virgins of the Middle East! "You can have sex but I can't," she whined, looking at the table and squirming in her seat.

"Who do you want to have sex with Eva?" I asked through the laughter. I grabbed her shoulder to get her attention and shook her jokingly.

"I am seeing my Economics professor at the university."

"Oh my God! Seriously?"

"Yes!" And she squirmed again. I could have sworn the bartender heard this pretty, young girl screaming out the word *sex* and so I dropped my voice and encouraged her to as well. He was whispering to his friend and pointing at her. "He's married so he takes me to his summer house and we have sex there." That was a lot of information to take in. I sipped my wine and widened my eyes to encourage her to continue. "Well, not real sex. He puts it in my ass so I don't break my virginity." *Great. Another anal story.* I had a student who was an older man, head of economics at the university. I hoped it wasn't him. I didn't want to have to deal with those mental pictures as I was teaching him how to construct an academic essay.

"He wants me to be his girl so he can have control over me but I just want the sex." She said 'sex' so that it came out very pronounced and it took me back to my primary school days, when some annoying kid in my class would run up to me, say 'sex' and run away. They knew they would get in trouble if someone heard them say it but they did it anyway to push the boundaries. Eva was pushing the boundaries of the norms of her society. Her whole family was. She had just got onto the topic of how great it would be if America invaded Syria because then there would be tons of hot soldiers for her to have sex with, when my thoughts started to veer off to Hassan and Saleh and after a couple more drinks, my eyes had welled up with tears and Eva noticed I was upset. I excused myself and went to the bathroom. Eva knew all about Saleh and I was grateful that she had given me a bit of space to pull myself together. In my tipsiness, I decided it would be a good idea to call him – something I never did anymore. Regardless of how he behaved, I still felt a love for him that kept me alive. It throbbed in my veins. The bathroom mirrors portrayed a lost woman on the outside, but inside I knew I was found if only I could connect to that spirit of *Love* again. I dialed his number. There were no sounds in the background, just the pumping of music on my end and the silence on his. They were both as loud as each other.

"What are you doing?" I asked, apprehensively. I heard nothing but silence. I pressed him to answer, panic forming in my chest ready to burst. Finally he said in a low voice,

"I'm at home in my room staring at the wall. I don't know what happened. I just found myself doing that." I burst into tears in a mixture of pain for him and frustration that I couldn't protect him. It all came flying out of my mouth. I didn't want to burden him and I hadn't meant to. It just happened before I knew it.

"Saleh no! Please! I'm so worried about you. I'm so worried."

I didn't know why I had assumed that emotions would get through to him because in the years we had known each other, it never had. He had never gone to hug me as I cried, or apologized for anything that affected my emotions. I felt like I was confronting emotions for him because he refused to encroach upon them himself. I felt like a conduit for pain: *his* pain. And as soon as I had that outburst, I knew he was gone.

That night I cried myself to sleep and dreamt. In that empty room where I lived, in that rickety house it stood out as a thing of beauty and was a sign that I was indeed, not alone. I was looking at a vision of a woman standing in pure whiteness and by her side was a green frog. The disembodied voice of a woman, whom I can only identify as being the Goddess herself, uttered these exact words:

"This woman needs the spiritual ways – her beliefs, her way of life as a spiritual person. But *you? You're* going straight to Heaven." I woke up, wondering what the frog represented and hoped what she had said was true because so far everything I had done in my life appeared to be a series of terrible mistakes.

Chapter 38

I had moved to a stunning shared house in the old city, now two months into my second stay in Syria I was working like crazy and was maintaining a good wage from private teaching. My friends said that people were broke because of the war but I just realized they were prioritizing and education was high on that list. Parents were eager to send their sons off to university so that they could get out of the country and be safe and I was one of a handful of native English speakers left in Damascus, qualified and knowledgeable regarding the exams they required. I didn't charge as much as I could have. Instead of exploiting my position, I just kept taking on more students until I had as many as fifteen at one time. That way I could keep my prices reasonable. Many of my students went off to university in Europe and America and I felt satisfaction at being able to help them get out of the country in a small way. I also set them up with a friend in London who ran a student visa program to assist them in obtaining temporary student visas. I am not a political person, but I am a teacher in spirit and I felt strongly that Syria was on the way to losing an entire generation to this emerging war. They would be forced to join the army, forced to abandon their education and be left with nothing to fall back on when the war was over. Whatever I could do in terms of preventing that, even for one person, I would be grateful. I felt blessed that I had been in the position to do this and when I cried at night because I was alone, I remembered the people I had assisted and kept safe from the clutches of the military and it held me up when all I wanted to do was sink.

Signs that Damascus was under threat from war emerged in December 2011. Bombs were detonated in central places of the city that were very busy. Buildings were destroyed such as the French hospital and some friends I had known before the unrest had been killed in those blasts. There were shootings in the old city that would come out of nowhere. My house was next to a police station and whenever there was an incident, I would notice that the police seemed more bewildered than anything else. And yet the Western media would have people believe that all of Assad's men were behind the violence. The protocol would involve the police shooting rifles up into the air in an attempt to warn people in the streets to go into their houses as danger was afoot. Adults and children would cry out in terror and rush indoors and sirens would blare throughout the neighborhood. And then gunfire would ring out and it seemed to go on forever. By Christmas, I had become used to hearing gunfights and the sound of bombs going off but it never stopped me from living life and I wasn't cowering in fear at home either. It was staggering to see how human beings cope within their environment, regardless of what horror they have to deal with on a daily basis. It bothered me more that guns and bombs sounded exactly like fireworks. I would have flashbacks of going to displays on bonfire night with my family and childhood friends, our hands dressed in gloves and our noses frozen with bitter winter weather. I would be given a sparkler lit by matches – I loved the smell of those and then I would write my name with the glittering, golden trail it left behind. My nan always made sure I had a sparkler on the fifth of November.

These sights and sounds would come flooding back to me at each explosion and then it would be followed by a deathly silence. Everyone would hold their breath and look at the person next to them as if to ask what that noise had been. And then I would perceive a bleak dread that spread a grey cloak of fear over my entire body. I felt like a magician's assistant. He would take that cloak and start from my toes and climb further and further until I disappeared from view leaving behind only the horror of every living being in that city. The terror of those around me was so strong it would take over my soul. Everything that happened during my time in Syria from here on out is set against a backdrop of bombs and gunfire: often far away but sometimes in the next street.

Then the new laws started. The government banned *iphones* because they were convinced that they could be used as a tool for spying. Then they banned every man under the age of thirty- five from leaving the country so that they could take a step toward conscription. But they couldn't keep it up because Assad's wealthy supporters were okay to watch a poor woman's son die in war, but were not willing to watch their own so they voted it out. In all, that law lasted twenty-four hours. Walking down the street became a unique experience. There were Russian and Chinese flags strung up in windows and I knew those people supported the regime because Russia and China were blocking Western intervention in Syria. They were also celebrated in rallies around Damascus, which I never attended despite being curious to see what was happening. I was still under suspicion of being a foreign journalist, undercover, gathering false information with the aim to stir trouble. My close friends were convinced that there was a foreign conspiracy against the country. Assad himself had used that wording on more than one occasion.

I understood that many people were in support of the regime and I saw where they were coming from with their stance, but these people were incredibly frustrating to talk to. I asked a student of mine what she would do if the situation became worse and America got involved and Syria became the next Iraq. The student just looked me dead in the face and said,

"There is nothing wrong. I will stay here. Everything is good. Everything is fine." The day before, a bomb had blown up the mall around the corner from her house. She had a young son to take care of. How was everything fine? Her answer was irritating and so I didn't pursue it anymore but I felt that if you truly had conviction in your beliefs, you would also be able to be realistic at the same time. That response was of someone living in Cuckoo Land. By the end of 2011, all talk of 'revolution' had ended within Syria itself and the truth about the civil war spreading from Homs, Hama and Aleppo, was out. Everyone was aware of the shockwaves echoing throughout that time worn land.

Chapter 39

It was a few days after Christmas and I was walking down the street in *Qassar*, the Christian quarter. This was where Sara used to take me every Christmas, to shop for decorations and look at the lights, but this year, windows were bare. There were no twinkling bulbs in reds, blues and greens blinking on trees and no giant blow-up snowmen and the shops played no Christmas music. Syria was in mourning for the many, many lives lost in cities around the country. There was nothing to celebrate.

My friend Nouman and I were sharing a bag of sweet popcorn and chatting about the weather because it looked as though snow was on the way, when he got a call. He pulled the phone out of his back pocket, handing me the popcorn to hold.

"One second," he said, apologetically.

"No worries! More popcorn for me!" I smirked, knowing it was his favorite food. I listened as he talked, by now understanding the majority of Arabic spoken around me. The first time I had lived there, my friends had all been expats but now I was always around Syrians. Picking up the language was inevitable.

“What? Have you spoken to her sister?” He said. I was alarmed. He sounded very concerned. Turning to me, he whispered,

“It’s Eva. That was her brother. She is missing and we think she has been arrested.”

Nouman, Eva and I had mutual friends and they started ringing his phone asking if he could help and if I had heard from her. He relayed the messages to me and I was saying I hadn’t. In fact the last I had heard, she was organizing a protest at Damascus University – but I didn't tell Nouman that in case. At times like this it’s hard to know whom to trust, constantly wondering who is against or for the president and who is with the secret police. I couldn't say anything in case I put her and her family in more danger. “Let me drop you home,” he said, phone balancing between his shoulder and his ear whilst he rummaged for his car keys, “I will drive down to see her dad and let you know what happens.”

“Can’t I come?” I asked.

“No. Her brother just said that soldiers barricaded the roads leading up to their place. Too many checkpoints round there.” I nodded my head in understanding. My heart was beating madly away in my chest as flashes of what might be happening to her if she had been arrested appeared before me like scenes from a twisted horror film. Nouman’s fear engulfed me as we drove home. Its long, cold fingers traced my spine. Her brother called again and told us that Eva had been missing for almost twenty-four hours. I wondered what on Earth happened to her. Did the police find out about her plans for the protest?

Questions continued to float around days later as we still had no word from her or from anyone who knew where she was and her family were distraught, her mother flying into my arms when it was finally safe enough for me to travel into the suburbs where they lived. It turned out that I was the only person with any knowledge of this protest Eva had texted me about. Her mother had suspected it but was glad for the confirmation and we spent the day sitting around in silence, phones at the ready and with vodka – redbulls in our hands. The brash TV channels calling out for revolution were on mute now – I was afraid this brave family had given up for good.

Chapter 40

It had been three weeks since Eva's mysterious disappearance and over three months since I had arrived back in Syria. The latter meant that I needed to renew my tourist visa. A friend took me to get my visa renewed at the ministry of interiors, something he had insisted upon as he had a friend who could *help* me. Syrian society bases a lot on who you know and what favors they can do for you. I could have just gone to the main public building I had visited in the first two weeks of my arrival for a stamp but no! My friend wanted to prove how *important* he was.

He took me to see a high-ranking man decorated with military awards that glinted arrogantly at me. His office was full of similar men who had all come in to take a look at the unmarried foreign girl – their smug smiles and words in Arabic made me feel sick.

"Why don't you come and teach my children?" Said one of them in good English. "At my house!" Deep laughter echoed throughout the office. I had to breathe deeply to contain my anger. "Yeah! Better yet, I need to improve my English! Come and *teach* me!"

A man strode over to lean against the boss' desk in front of me and look me up and down with a look of disgust and lust on his face. I didn't expect this mixture of perverted digs and hostility – it appeared to be the kind of harassment reserved for women only by those Arab men in a position of power. My friend spoke, a fake smile on his face. He wasn't stupid. He knew what they were suggesting.

"She is worried because she wants to stay here longer but her stamp has run out. She doesn't want to get in trouble and..." he added hesitantly, "She will probably be engaged to my friend soon." A smart move that allowed me to breathe again so I smiled at him in an unspoken gesture of thanks. Arrogant twat shifted a little in his seat at this new turn of events and leaning-against- desk-prick, got up and took a seat near the door to smoke. Twat then proceeded to brush off my concerns about my visa having passed its expiry date. In fact he laughed at me saying,

"You don't need a visa! If any soldier stops you, tell them they must call me!"

His laughter boomed out like an evil genius and the other six suits in the room joined in. He was tall and that made him more frightening to me. The air of authority about him was undeniable. When he had to take a phone call, he retained his hungry smile and kept glancing my way. Uncomfortable but there for a reason, I immediately turned to my friend and whispered urgently with a rising panic in my voice,

"No way! What if he forgets who I am! I can't, not have a visa in my passport! I will be arrested!"

In the end, after some delicate pressing, arrogant twat did send us to the public immigration building and they stamped my visa. I could stay. To be honest, I didn't have much choice in the matter because I had many students who were relying on me to get them into university outside Syria and I am a teacher. I don't abandon my students no matter what life throws at me.

I was celebrating my renewed visa with Poppy, who I realized, still had no idea that a war had started up in Syria because she wasn't allowed to leave the house without her husband.

"Poppy…" I had said to her cautiously, "You do realize that this isn't Saudi or Egypt right? Syrian wives here go out like anyone else would."

"Really… are you sure? My husband said it was dangerous and that I could get kidnapped or something."

I had just smiled and nodded. I knew another Western woman who had married a Syrian and he had told her the same thing. As is always the way, her worst fears came true on the very first day she decided to come out with me (after much persuasion) without her husband tagging along. She had already been in the country for two years and was waiting for her Syrian husband to be granted an American passport through marriage when I said she should come with me to a shopping center in *Mezze.* Although nervous, as soon as we had stepped on the side of the main road to hail a taxi, she flagged one down with a chirpy American,

"Taxi please driver!" A man stopped his yellow cab on the other side of the road, his face peered through his open window at us and I was reminded of a hyper dog on a car journey. I didn't want to cause her alarm and make her feel stupid for taking the initiative to seize a free cab so I chose to ignore the disembodied woman's voice that distinctly said the word *NO,* right in my ear. If my intuition could speak, that's how it would sound because I have never heard it say anything before I have only been able to *feel* warnings. But we got in anyway and now he was driving us out to fields and villages beyond the concrete jungle that is *Mezze*. In the years I have lived in Damascus, I have never had any problems with taxi drivers so this was a confusing turn of events for me. As he drove I observed that I had never even known these places beyond the city existed. My friend was crying and screaming until the driver, with a psychotic grin plastered across his stupid face, let us out in the middle of absolutely nowhere. In fact it looked like we were in a medieval village. A woman came over to us and was so kind. She comforted my friend while I got hold of contacts that could send us a taxi to get us out of there. I felt sorry for my friend after that, whose fears her husband had instilled in her had become so great that they materialized into an actual experience. That was definitely, Sara and I had decided, *The Law of Attraction* at its worst so with that memory in mind, I didn't try to get Poppy to leave the house. With her naivety, it probably was the best place for her.

She was making me some pancakes when I got a phone call from Eva's sister telling me to come round right away. She was speaking too quickly in Arabic and I couldn't understand her properly so I asked her to put her brother on the phone.

"Eva is here," he said, slowly as though he were trying to comprehend the very words he was speaking. "Come and see us. My mum is asking for you." I hung up the phone, not wanting to waste a second and kissed Poppy goodbye.

"Darling I have to go! I might come back later once I figure out what's happening. Remember the girl I told you about who went missing? She's been found."

"Lemme know you're safe. Text me later," Poppy replied with a concerned tone. I later deliberated over whether she might know more than she was letting on about the situation in Syria.

"Will do," I shouted back, grabbing my handbag and slamming the door behind me and thinking how lucky I was to have met such great people in that city.

As I made my way to Eva's place in a beat-up yellow taxi, my heart was in my mouth and my palms were sweating like crazy. What was I going to see when I got there? Was Eva even alive? I had been praying and had organized a candlelight vigil with our large group of mutual friends, in hopes for her safe return. I didn't know what else to do. Now I was about to see if *Love* had heard our calls for help.

“It’s Tina.” I called into the intercom outside their front gate. Through the bars I saw her brother treading quickly downstairs. He kissed me hello on both cheeks and led me up. Their front door opened up into their living room and sitting on the sofa was Eva. She didn't look any different, except she had noticeably lost weight. The bright pink blusher she was wearing on her face only highlighted how sallow it had become whilst blue pencil emphasized eyes that, like Saleh’s, were nothing but pools of black now. Shadows lurked there and it was frightening to see.

“Eva? Where have you been? We have been so fucking worried…” I hesitated over whether I should hug her but she jumped to her feet and laughed – an empty laugh and I was caught off guard.

“I’m okay Tina. Don't make a fuss.” Someone shoved vodka and pineapple into my hand and hers and her family left us alone, I presumed to catch up. I wasn't sure. I was confused. “Listen, I went to a protest – it was last minute. Not thought through and I got caught. That’s it. I was so stupid.” I was relieved that she was trying to act normal – I didn't know if that was for my benefit or hers. I asked,

"Stupid?"

"Yes. I was stupid because I was protesting – not because I was caught!" She laughed loudly and I jumped, not expecting it.

"Okay…" I replied when I had gathered my composure. "So you think protesting is stupid." She downed the rest of her hefty drink in one swig and I could only sit, staring at her. Where was the Eva I knew, who called for revolution and ousting the president?

"I was arrested okay…" She whispered, seeing that I hadn't been convinced thus far. "And the police spoke to me and now I know it was wrong. It was stupid and wrong and I don't think anyone should protest. Look at what the president has done for us?" She swung her arms around to indicate the room, the house and the city. "We should be grateful for what we have." I nodded but when I am finding it hard to believe someone I have a habit of staring them in the eyes, as if I am trying to find the truth in them and Eva noticed. "I am fine Tina! Stop! I have been in jail but I am out now and I am fine." I apologized and hugged her, wondering if this 'I am fine' spiel was reserved for the foreigner but I didn't care. I was just very glad she was safe now. We downed more vodka, and put on MTV. Drunk, I called Nouman from the taxi later that night.

"What do you think happened to her… in there…?" I could barely get the words out. It was with a morbid curiosity that I asked. He seemed to take a long time to answer.

"Oh the usual. Maybe rape, possibly torture. Or maybe she was just locked up with another group of women. I've heard some stories myself but my advice to you is not to think about these things too much. Just be there for Eva if she needs to speak." I was relieved. It was good advice.

Chapter 41

My heart was pinging along with my phone. Saleh was texting me again and I was in a state of sublime happiness. It had been three and a half months since we had spoken and I had finally managed to let him go, but now all the love I had been directing toward him had finally been received. He was in the middle of telling me how much he missed me. I didn't know what had instigated this U-turn inside him – all I wanted was to see his beautiful face again.

“I am coming to get you,” he said, his voice gruff but light-hearted as was his way. “So be ready in thirty minutes.” Before I hung up I gave him directions to my new place as I had moved once more to a big flat of my own in *Jasr Al abiyad* – a posh area near several government buildings that was not suffering the power cuts I had been getting in my previous place. I had spent most of the past couple of months making more money than I had earned at the British school back in 2009 but rising city rents, meant I was just keeping my head afloat even if I was able to finally afford a nice place just for me. The government had started turning the electricity for the city off for three hours, every three hours. I always assumed I would never be able to cope without hot water and heating in my home but I got on with it like everybody else. To keep warm on freezing winter nights, we would all gather in local restaurants that had generators. The city was abuzz with the sound of them whirring all through the day.

I rushed to look nice for Saleh, fiddling with straightening my hair and make-up. He wanted to go to a restaurant in the Old city but I felt sick to my stomach with nerves. I was nauseous with anticipation, wondering how he would behave towards me. Sometimes he could be moody, sometimes gentle, but often abrupt and I was feeling a little tender to be honest. For the past couple of weeks I had really let the stress of living in a city at war get to me. I was now, from what we knew, the only qualified, native English speaking teacher left in Damascus as several foreigners had recently left the country and people were relying on me to help fight the war with books and pens. A charity run by two Australians was training nineteen year olds for exams that would gain them scholarships to universities abroad and they had somehow got my number and called to ask if I would consider sticking around a little longer to help teach the kids. I felt that I couldn't say no and anyway I had truly wanted to make sure those kids had the chance to get a good education without the backdrop of bombs and the constant threat to their lives.

I was worried about Eva who was now in hospital after having an emotional breakdown and wasn't eating. The memories of what happened to her in jail had overwhelmed her and she couldn't cope. She told me she had been beaten several times as well as starved for days. The fear that people I loved might also be locked up would stop my heart and I was worried to death about it. It was like suffocating under water.

I lost my friend Faruk who had collected me from the airport on my first day back. He had texted me to check if I was free to talk and I had told him I was busy – I was working on a lesson plan. He wished me good luck with it, in his gentle manner but I just felt frustrated at the interruption. The lesson plan was turning out to be more complex than I had expected. The next night I got a call from Malak, an old student and mutual friend of Faruk.

"Do you remember Faruk?" She asked slowly, through tears. I was confused. Of course I did.

"I just texted with him yesterday. I've seen him since I've been here," I answered. "Why?"

"He's been killed in a car bomb just outside his house in the Old city. I can't believe it. So, so sad." She cried. All I could do was put my head in my hands and shake it over and over. Malak continued. "I thought I should tell you because I saw it on the news and I know you can't understand formal Arabic. Let me know if you need anything. Oh and be careful Tina. We can't know when the next car bomb might strike."

I threw my phone onto the floor and heard it smash apart. I had been too busy to talk to him and now he was dead. He didn't often text or call me because he had a girlfriend and it would have been inappropriate so the fact that he just happened to want to speak then, was horrific and I was consumed with guilt, wondering what our last words to each other may have been. After that, the threat of car bombs going off around the city was too great to ignore so I took to sleeping awkwardly on my small sofa, too afraid to get into my bed located under windows pointing towards a main road. If the windows or wall had exploded inwards due to a bombing, I could have been severely injured. Although it was safer, the sofa had messed up my spine and one morning I stretched the wrong way, locking the muscles in my neck to the point where I couldn't move at all for several hours. When good, reliable Ahmad came round to take me to the hospital, I was prescribed muscle relaxers by the doctor and after trying the first one, I liked it. Those pills relaxed every muscle – it was like getting a massage, not just on my body but my mind too. After taking one I couldn't think or feel. I forgot about the mess my life was in, my failures at finding and keeping love, my inability to truly find God. Sometimes I looked back at what was left of my notebook and at all the bits of 'wisdom' written there and recall the way I had felt those writings were the answers to my doubts and worries. I often convinced myself that they weren't answers to incorporate into my life at all but little drops of insight that were *meant* to disappear, like a *Snapchat* photo, as fast as they had come. After all, I had been in Syria for about five months now and I was still making mistakes – not the actions of a woman who had found the truth of love, life and death.

There was the sound of a car horn outside and so I grabbed my bag and ran down the echoing staircase to Saleh who was parked in front of my building. It was evident that we were both pleased to see each other as we held hands and hugged for a long time. I saw that his eyes looked older, his frame, slimmer. His fingers that caressed mine were thinner and more worn out. The war was sitting heavily on the Syrian people and it was upsetting to see.

As we got stuck in a long line of traffic on *Straight Street*, I could sense him staring at me. I frowned back, puzzled.

"What's the difference between caring about someone and loving them?" He finally said. I was bewildered. In three years I had never heard him employ this soft tone with me. It was a question spoken with a warm heart. His defenses were down and I realized that he was afraid of losing me. He didn't want me to leave his life for good but in what capacity he wanted me soon became apparent.

“Well that obviously means you don't love the person.” I replied, concealing the hurt in my voice and placing my hand on his thigh. But he wouldn't allow me to interpret his words in that way.

“I do care for you. It’s the same as love,” he insisted. All I could do was wonder why he didn't just say he loved me then. He wanted me but he didn't want to commit to me; that much was obvious. After everything I had been through, I didn't care. I just wanted to be near him again, to soak him in and breathe love and passion for him and him alone.

“Let’s go and have dinner.” Saleh said, spotting a space and parking in it. My soul soaring, I followed him into our favorite restaurant. I ordered falafel and chips and asked for some bread, seeing that our basket was empty but the waiter just shook his head and informed us that they hadn’t been able to get hold of any that day. By now this was a regular occurrence in Damascus, with some shops unable to get hold of this staple.

His friend met us later and as we laughed and joked with him, Saleh put his hand firmly on my knee. He whispered to me, poking fun at his friend and tried to make me laugh all night. And as we left the restaurant, he placed his hand around my shoulders, something he had never done before; I felt like the luckiest woman on Earth. This man who was so strong and brave, cared for me. He didn't love me but he saw worth where he had previously seen nothing and I allowed his attention to carry me away to

Heaven.

Getting in the car to make our way home, we were still laughing at his funny friend. We were reminiscing about the cat we had shared – a time we had gone to eat and took the kitten in the car with us – when I saw some books with English writing laying in the back seat. Reading them brought me back to Earth with a massive bang and I almost died inside. They were books students require to practice for the English exams I was teaching.

"Ah yeah. I was meaning to ask. I need you to help me pass so I can apply to university in Europe. What do you think?" He said, following my line of sight. I swallowed hard and pretended to be on top of the world.

"Of course I will."

When we reached my building, he undid his seatbelt and clambered out of the car, his large body and long legs, bending awkwardly to fit through the door. It looked as though he was coming upstairs with me and I felt a mixture of apprehension and excitement. It had been a long time – I wanted to be with him but at the same time I hated the aftermath of feeling empty afterwards. I looked up and into his dark eyes as he asked me for my door key and I knew I wouldn't be able to say no to him. I belonged to him. As his big frame settled onto my Syrian sized sofa, he looked like a giant and I couldn't help but giggle to myself. I remembered when he had been called to register for military service. He said that he and a group of young men had to be sorted into various roles. When the boss called him into the decision room, he took one look at the size of him and put him into Special Forces. That and the fact that he had to order his shoes from abroad – a UK size twelve – made him significantly larger than the average Syrian man.

"You look enormous on that couch Saleh!" I sniggered. "But you do look as though you have lost a bit of weight."

"Yeah? Well… I'm just stressed about my family. My dad wants me to leave but I am refusing. I want to stay and fight with the Free Syrian Army!" It was a serious topic but as usual with me he had his guard up and tried to make a joke of it instead. He started jumping up and down, pretending to shoot with an AK47. I sat on a chair at my dining table until he came over, took my hand and led me into the bedroom.

"You are very beautiful tonight," he murmured, getting under the sheets on my bed. "My friend said you are the prettiest foreign girl he's seen. He said I'm a lucky man!" He laughed, looking pleased with himself. As I turned to take off my top I screwed up my face thinking how his friend was funny but that I couldn't see him that way. It occurred to me that I wouldn't *choose* to sleep with him. *Choose*, I repeated in my mind. *Choose*? I wondered why that word came to mind like that and why I felt so perplexed by it. Surely it's common knowledge that we choose whom we sleep with and that we aren't attracted to everyone. Saleh continued to ramble on. “You’re hot. We were both saying how hot you are when you went to the bathroom. I was proud of myself!”

Now, most people, on hearing this would welcome the apparent compliment to their appearance but *oh no, not me* – I had to make things more complicated! I was on a search for the truth after all. I noticed that if I pushed the ego boost aside, I was left with a feeling of being objectified that didn't leave me during sex. I had thought for the past couple of years that Saleh was sleeping with me because he loved me and that the act represented his love for me but in reality hadn’t he just been attracted to my body? Wasn't he just out to get something? Like pleasure, self-esteem, attention? And wasn't I out to get that from him too? As a witch I had been certain that sex served a spiritual purpose but isn’t it just leading us down the wrong path? We think it is the act of joining two souls but in reality it is the joining of two bodies, which only further perpetuates the idea that we are our physical forms.

As Saleh got ready to go home, I felt worse than I ever had before. Not because he was leaving after sex again or because I was sure he was using me, but because I felt guilty. I had objectified him all this time. I had seen him as a body, when really underneath it all he is a spirit, equal in beauty with every other spirit. *And hadn’t I accused him of wanting me around only for sex in the past when in reality, it is I who also wanted him for sex?*

I recalled. *Hadn't I wanted him to prove he had chosen me by sleeping with me?*

I further felt guilty towards my brother, his friend, whom I had dismissed because his appearance was not pleasing in my opinion. *How strange*, I thought, *to think this way*. I was so lost in thought that I forgot to call out a goodbye to Saleh as he made his way out the door. It was three in the morning but now that this knowledge had dawned on me, I was wide-eyed and more alert than ever. It was a sign that I was on to something. I pondered; *this isn't just about sex. This is about relationships with one person too. It all goes back to the same thing – they both serve the notion that we are all spirits that are separate from each other. Choosing one person to love emotionally, spiritually and physically is not the way to peace.* And then it came to me and I sat up straight in my chair, looking straight up and out through the window, into the night sky where the stars reminded me of something. *I think sex is the attempt to try to recreate our oneness with each other.* I played back all the intimate moments I had experienced with Saleh in my mind. The Egyptian caretaker flashed up and the way he had terrorized me instilled the same fear in me that he had back then. My muscles tensed in remembrance of the time I had been stalked in the streets and those men who had tried to force me into their car and I decided it was time to stop having revelations and rest.

My neck injury was aggravating me so after taking a quick shower, I downed a muscle relaxer to help me sleep and when I woke up in the morning I wondered what would happen if I took another. I had seen the truth of my misguided relationship with Saleh and it had left me feeling ashamed. Not only had I been pursuing illusions that hurt me but I had hurt others, especially him in the process, which was the last thing I would ever have wanted to do. Deep down inside I knew it signified the end of us for once we have seen the light we can't pretend we haven't. Instead of rejoicing in my newfound awareness, I tried to delay its impact by relying on the muscle relaxer pills to help me forget.

That meant using the pills to get me through the days when I wasn't with students: my private students, the kids at the charity and now *Saleh*. I didn't want to think about how unhappy I was and how Saleh had only got back in touch so that I would teach him and how I had imagined us being back together had taken me to Heaven. It hadn't – because my love for him was dependent on him fulfilling the perfect vision. When the books on the backseat proved our relationship was nothing but an illusion, all the love disappeared and was replaced with pain and anger. I knew from all of my interactions with the Divine so far that love couldn't disappear. So what was true? The love that is eternal or the love I treasure for this one person that's very existence can be threatened by the smallest of things? I was too busy drugging myself up until I was akin to a zombie to think anymore about it.

Chapter 42

Whenever I would tell a Syrian woman that I was in a relationship with a Syrian man, they would look at me with pity. Bambi eyes would look my way concealed under thick, black lashes and a smile would form at the corners of glossy, red mouths in a display of smugness. I knew exactly what they were thinking. *He's using you for sex; Poor, silly, English girl. Do you really think a Syrian man could love you? Things are different here in Syria.* I was sitting at a dining table with one such woman. I was giving her a private lesson on formal letter writing but we had got onto the topic of marriage and I had mentioned Saleh and her normally friendly tone had taken on a self-righteous air. In almost three years of mingling with the people of Syria, she was the only one who verbalized what everyone had been thinking all along.

"He can't marry you." I looked at the floor feeling nauseous. I had been addicted to the muscle relaxers for a few weeks now and I wished I had them with me.

"This is what Arabic men do. They find a woman to have a relationship with – for sex – and they marry a serious girl." Although I knew she was just telling me the truth of the matter, I felt like she was attacking me. She used the words "serious girl" but she should just have said "a girl who isn't a whore".

"You're too old for him" she continued. Her words sounded like shattering glass or was it just the bombing and shooting outside? "An Arabic man must marry a girl who is younger than him. She must be a virgin." I didn't dare to look her in the eye in case she should see that I wasn't. I was in denial, trying desperately to protect myself from the hurt creeping up on me.

"Saleh is making a joke out of you." I didn't know what her intentions were but I was sure it revolved around her having one over on an English girl, whose beauty, *she felt* surpassed her own, whose education *she felt* was superior to her own and whose freedoms *she felt* were more abundant than her own. I had wondered many times why there was such an atmosphere of competition amongst Arabic women. And why against me when it was obvious that I was not considered to be marriage material? It was the same for the many Syrian women who had ever greeted me with false smiles, who had crooned that they had missed me when I wasn't their teacher anymore and who would tell me I looked nice but would whisper to their friends as soon as my back was turned. It all came back to me in a rush of frustration, hurt and hatred. But as is my way, when I had gathered enough composure to breathe and move again, I looked at the time and informed my student that we had twenty minutes left to go.

"Let's look at this list of endings for a letter. Which ones do you think are suitable to use with a formal text?"

As soon as I got home, I emptied my boxes of muscle relaxers into the toilet. I am not sure why but I became clear thinking for the first time since I had arrived back in Syria and although I was crushed by the honesty of my student, something was stirring that told me I had almost completed my journey. No matter what pain I felt from here, I knew I could deal with it – a light had been switched on and it wasn't about to go out. People often ask me what the catalyst was behind why I decided to leave Syria when I did. I might nod along when they assume it was because of the escalating war or make up some family or money issue. The absolute truth is that it was the words of this woman that forced me to retire from the mission I was on. I realized it was a misguided mission that had now done all the good it could do for those around me. It was time to look inwards and notice the recurring themes in my life.

I hadn't been able to shake the revelation I had experienced where I recognized that everything I had done had been an attempt to recreate the oneness inherent to myself and my brothers and sisters and thinking of it brought a lot of peace. It meant that there was a higher purpose to everything I have ever done in my life – I just hadn't been aware of it until now. From wanting to belong in Syrian society, to having sexual relationships and special relationships, to the whole reason for my spiritual quest to begin with, all of it has been the chasing of a long forgotten memory. In the mundane moments of my life, when I was positive I had forgotten my mother-father God, I was in fact searching for him, in the eyes of Ryan, Saleh even Sara and everyone around me I was close with.

As I stood on my balcony after returning home from my student's house that evening and looked out over a Syria at war, I wished I had *A Course in Miracles* with me. I couldn't decide if I had done well without it or whether I had made a mistake in leaving it behind. Unrelenting gunfire stilled my heart like sudden visions of Ryan, safe and sound back in London. Recollections of my old self, all those years ago who was so innocent drifted through my mind and I couldn't believe the difference between her and the Tina standing there that day: silver roots waiting to burst through my hair and wrinkles on my brow. But tonight, I didn't criticize. I maintained that I looked beautiful and savored all the pain I was feeling in that moment, after all, it was assuring me that I was still alive, that I had lived and most importantly that I had loved. I had to go back to London now, I knew. However, first I needed answers and there was one last hope.

Chapter 43

Strangely enough convent life had always appealed to me. It was a shelter from the storm. A place with law and order and structure; absent from chaos. A woman who joined a convent had no choice but to become spirit. She has no Earthly possession, unable to meet the needs of her body except food, light and warmth and most of all, primal woman was banned. There was no doubt that my Primal woman had got me into a lot of trouble. She made me outspoken, which probably wouldn't go down well with the nuns. They would probably make me do a vow of silence. Primal woman made me intuitive but they would cast me out and say it was 'witchcraft.' They might exorcise me. Worst of all, Primal woman made me *feel.* I was convinced my feelings were the root of my problems. Over the past six months I had been *feeling* against my will or so I thought. Those nuns would look at me with pity and disgust that my feelings had led me to give to anyone but God. I wanted all of these aspects of myself to disappear. I wanted to start again and be reborn.

I made the trip to Saydnaya church and convent by minibus. Saleh and his friends couldn't believe it when they heard I had travelled there alone and on a mode of transport reserved for the 'little people'. I would have taken public transport more often in Syria but I was always stared at by men, women and children, to the point where I once snapped and offered a couple of *starers* some popcorn to make their watching experience more enjoyable. No one could believe that I would risk the journey outside of Damascus at that time either. There were many checkpoints along the road and if the bus had been stopped they would have demanded identification from everyone and as I only had a British passport, who knows what may have happened to me. I was calm though and just hoped for the best.

Just a few weeks before, men calling for 'democracy' had shot at the church but miraculously none of the shells exploded. There were many stories of strange occurrences in and around Saydnaya that have been purported to be 'miracles'. Luckily, I believed in those! Sadly, the shooting in Saydnaya reflected a disturbing new twist in the conflict. Religious tensions were rife. Muslims hated Christians because many were seen to be in support of the regime. Shiites and Sunnis hated the Alawites because they assumed they were in support of the President from the same sect of Islam. Disturbingly enough, this tension was being played out between the average Syrian. I knew many people who had commented on their newfound hatred for Christians. I also had a student whose best friend of twenty years had been sending her death threats because she was an Alawi (the same sect of Islam as the president) and 'obviously hated democracy.'

It was absurd and so sad that God’s name had entered into this conflict that had nothing to do with him. The Syria I had known and loved – the spiritual Syria – was dying.

Luckily, the journey was uneventful and as I got out of the bus I looked around me at the mighty mountains. The place I was going was located at the very top. The sun was stronger here than it was in the city and it beat down on me as I climbed the many stairs that led to the convent of our lady of Saydnaya. The stoney color of the convent walls blinded me as the sun sparkled off of them. Ironically, the place looked like magic. Then the bells started going and the nun I was waiting for appeared, shuffling out of the tiny door that was the entrance to this magnificent time honored church. She didn’t smile as I greeted her and she didn't look me in the eyes, but I was expecting it. I had been there often enough with Sara to know that most of those nuns maintained the appearance of miserable old hags! She said her name was Maria and she showed me the canteen, kitchen and orphanage, which housed about twenty children. I loved teaching children and wanted to introduce myself but the nun ushered me out of there quickly. We walked along a winding terrace over the side of the mountain. This church was really high up. I could see for miles over the fields and mountainous terrain below. It was a stunning view. My room dazzled me too. I was led through double doors that opened into a stone-floored space.

The walls were painted a calming sky-blue. The bed frame was pure white and the wardrobe was crisp white. There were Persian rugs of many colors piled up in the corner and gorgeous handmade blankets in layers on my bed in case I got cold. I had private balcony space outside my room and a chair so I could do what I had come for: to contemplate *Love.*

"Give it to me," the nun spoke for the second time. I turned my attention to look at her hardened face. She pointed roughly at my belongings and said it again. "Give it to me. Quick!"

"I'm sorry? Give you what?" I replied with a mixture of emotions. I wasn't sure if I should be angry, scared or polite.

"Your bag. No make-up, no nice clothes. You wear the same as me." My eyes widened. I didn't know this was part of the deal. "Come on. I have to make dinner." I hesitated. *I need my make-up and oh my God. I have naturally curly hair. I need my straighteners. I can't go around with curly hair*, I thought briefly before she grabbed the bag from my hands and started rummaging through it, leaving only my underwear, notebook and toothbrush.

"Dinner will be ready soon. Have a bath and wash that stuff off your face. When you come down to the canteen I want to see the real you. Clothes are in the closet." I watched, mortified as she closed the door behind her. I weighed up my options and it was obvious that I didn't have much say in the matter. I couldn't go home now as I would need to take a bus and I didn't know which one to get. It might be late by the time they start running. We all knew it was more dangerous in the dark in a country at war.

Reluctantly I ran the water in the spotless, en-suite tub and got in. I had only been able to shower so far in Damascus so it was nice to bathe, even if I was about to resemble a scarecrow for the next few weeks. I scrubbed my arms and legs with the milk and honey soap provided. There was the famous Damascene olive soap for my hair – I couldn't imagine anything worse. Soap made my hair so dry. Looking at the dark green bar I was reminded of the symbolic nature of witchcraft. I wanted to wash all the residue sadness away from the past few years of my life, convincing myself it had been the inability to understand that had landed me where I was today. I wanted to understand why there was a war in Syria and why I had returned. I wanted to know why Hassan had to go and why Saleh couldn't love me. I rubbed the soap into my scalp vigorously and smiled to myself. I wanted to wash away all the thoughts that don't serve me. I washed my face – around my eyes and my lips – to cleanse what I saw and renew what I spoke. I was determined to get the answers here.

As the nun had requested my presence at dinner, I imagined that she wanted to speak to me, maybe give me some spiritual guidance. In actuality, nobody spoke to me and nobody even acknowledged my existence. I nibbled at dinner by myself in the corner and kept trying to catch somebody's eye. I wondered if they didn't know I was a guest at the convent because I was wearing the same scratchy black wool skirt with an unflattering heavy black top that weighed down on my shoulders and aggravated my neck injury. I looked just like them, except messier because my horrid curly hair had sprung up rather than hung down and I looked like a clown. It really bothered me to look like all the others in the room. I was used to being pounced upon as the exciting foreigner and getting all the attention. Now I was nobody special and David's words and Jesus' words came rushing back to me. If I still wanted to be different, I hadn't truly embraced the teachings in the book yet. I went back to my room, praying to *Love* to help me work harder. I put all my energy into trying to change the past, wishing, *if only Saleh hadn't used me and led me on I wouldn't be here now. If it wasn't for him I would be back in London, not stuck with these mean nuns.* I was so frustrated at him.

That night I looked out at the kaleidoscope of colors that was nearby towns perched on mountains surrounding Damascus. I had wrapped my pashmina around me and sat on the rickety chair that had been placed outside my room on my terrace. All I had to talk to was *Love*. A symphony of sadness played in the distance. Gun fights and bombing. How far or how near it was I didn't know. I only knew that the sounds were echoing off the mountains. It seemed cruel that the sounds would be amplified for the people of Damascus.

By now, the relaxed atmosphere of the capital city was fading. I knew I would be leaving Syria very soon. I dreaded that day because it would be the day when my heart would be ripped in two and when I would have to give up for good. I would never be able to return to this country ever again. When *Love* lived in Syria it was in the togetherness of the people, but now many had succumbed to an illusion of separation. For the regime or against the regime: Christian, Alawi, Sunni, Shiite: Democracy or Dictatorship: Rich or poor: Protest or rally. I remembered being told off on my second day in Syria in 2009 by a shopkeeper in the Old City. Fascinated by the rich spiritual history of the country, I had asked him in innocence, what religion he was. His face dropped and turned somber.

"Never ask a Syrian person this question," he had said. He frowned at me and stood up to look me in the eye. He had an aura of peace around him despite looking so annoyed. "Us Syrians live side by side. We are many religions and we respect everyone regardless of faith."

I had immediately started to apologize and explain that I was new to his beautiful land and I didn't realize, but he interrupted me by holding out his hands. They seemed to radiate a warmth.

"It is simply that we don't care about differences because we all love the same God and with his love, he teaches us to love each other." Then I saw his Qu'ran on the table. I was stunned by these words of wisdom and dropped my head in shame as I left his shop, understanding that the world would be a better place if we all stopped labeling each other by our religion.

It was a Syrian person who had taught me that labeling people was a form of separation from God and from each other and now it was Syrian people who had succumbed to it. On my first night at the convent, I prayed that the people fighting would remember they were one in the eyes of *Love.* Of course I knew that it was all easy to think and feel from the point of view of an outsider because it wasn't my family being killed. So the next day at breakfast I tried to talk to the nuns about it but they were unwelcoming. I asked if I could join a lone woman at her table.

"No thank you sister Maria," she said. I managed an awkward laugh.

"Oh my name is Tina, not Maria. My fault I should have…" I tried to explain. She didn't even look up from her toast as she said,

"I am eating, sister Maria." I stood in shock for a few seconds before forcing myself to dump my tray on the nearest table and head up to my room with a bread roll and some jam. *This place is weird*, I thought. *Flippin' nutters*! As I sat on the edge of my bed eating, I scratched at the back of my knees. The itchy skirt had given me some kind of rash. I wished I had my own clothes and made a mental note to ask whichever nun was in charge, if I could have them back.

"Excuse me," I said, later that day, tapping the shoulder of a nun who was looking out on Damascus from the roof terrace. She turned to look at me and she was wearing what looked like a cardigan of mine over her black top. My expressive face must have looked a picture as I recognized my item of clothing.

"What do you want, sister Maria?" She said, not angry – more irritated. I was so afraid. Everything was confusing me and I dealt with that by running away from that nun as fast as I could and barricading myself in my room until dinner time.

To top it all off, two other nuns addressed me as sister Maria that week and it was driving me mad. I am Tina. I am from London. I am thirty years old. I am a teacher. I am not sister Maria. And then I caught myself trying to separate again. I had a brief argument with myself regarding whether the teachings from *A Course in Miracles* could actually be applied to real life. *What if I am in danger? What if this is a crazy cult? What if they brainwash me?* And then I disputed over whether this was my attempt to hold onto the idea of being separate. I figured that the most logical explanation was that they had given me some kind of nun name. The strange part was though, that I had heard other nuns being called the same thing! I tried to brush it off by telling myself that I had never been to a convent before so I wouldn't know how one worked. *Maybe it is normal.*

When I had calmed down I went over my predicament. *How am I going to talk to these people?* I thought. *They dedicated their lives to God and are better than me in every way. Surely they would have answers?* I was aware that it was strange for someone who had identified as a witch to be so interested in convent life and I was pretty certain that they wouldn't be so interested in me if they had known what spiritual background I came from. A few witches I knew back home had an ingrained hatred of all religion as they were brought up and forced to attend church and read the Bible. For me though, I'd seen the statues of Mother Mary with offerings of fruit and flowers at her feet and I saw little difference between her and the Goddess herself. As the Syrian shopkeeper had taught me, religion is just another way to separate us from each other. Take every opportunity to look for the similarities between us as opposed to the differences – I had spent enough time looking for differences. Even labeling myself as a witch was starting to feel wrong because I am always going to meet people who aren't witches, like a Christian is always going to meet people who aren't Christian. I knew for a fact too that life would have been so much brighter had I focused on how alike Syrian women were to me rather than how different. I would have been freed from jealous thoughts, feelings of unworthiness and lack. What I didn't get was if God says I can live peacefully by eliminating ideas of difference between myself and other people from my thoughts, why was I clinging to them as though my life depended on it when in reality my freedom was dependent on letting go.

Chapter 44

On my seventh day at the convent, I heard an unexpected knock on my door and standing there was a very smiley nun who spoke fluent English. She gestured for me to follow and started pointing out some features of the building that I hadn't noticed before. She showed me the image on the stairs – a stain in the shape of the Virgin Mary. She told me about the miracle of the unexploded shells the month before. I was surprised and listened with interest yet when I tried to ask her why nobody would speak to me, she gave me the impression that she hadn't heard my question.

The nun led me into a room where more nuns where sitting in front of the desk of the Mother Superior. Everyone had big smiles on their similar faces. With amazement, I watched as their small eyes flashed hazel and their button noses scrunched up in a display of happiness. Everyone looked eerily similar. But I didn't have time to think about it because they were acting like I had passed some secret test. A chair was vacated for me and I sat on it, feeling nervous as well as slightly amused. These women looked back at me as though I were their daughter and instantly I fell in love with them all. They asked me questions about my life back in England and I answered honestly. They didn't speak of religion. Just hope for a better future for Syria. They got out some textbooks and asked if it was true that I had been a teacher at the British school a few years ago. I was amazed to learn that they had been students there at one time. I had never taught nuns before. Surely they had more to teach me! They talked about their English classes some more and then I seized the opportunity to change the topic. I wanted to make use of the time I had at the convent. A week had already gone by.

"I want to be a nun." Everyone fell quiet and they nodded their heads as if they were remembering their own callings. "I want to be like you," I said again.

"Are you Catholic?" Asked one.

They already knew I wasn't. That wasn't going to work. I squinted my eyes at a ray of sunshine escaping through blinds hanging over arched windows and shook my head.

"But I love God too!" I was aware that I sounded like a child; one who didn't understand how the rules of the world work but I didn't care. I wanted so badly to just live for God – I wasn't 'good' at living life. Everything seemed to go wrong all the time and some part of me thought I now knew *too much* about myself in a way. Knowing sex and relationships have not satisfied my soul, how will I be able to settle back into normal life ever again? Visions of myself as a TEFL victim or a crazy cat lady came to mind and I flinched. I didn't want to be lonely forever. I was lonely enough as it is at the age of thirty – was that my destiny? The Mother Superior sat next to me and put her hand on my knee.

"Maria. God loves you too but this isn't the place for you. You are young. You have much to learn and that learning must take place among people." A young nun with a sweet smile placed a cup of tea in front of me and then picked it up and handed it to me. She had such love in her eyes as she wrapped her fingers around mine so that I would grip the cup. I sensed a deep connection to these beautiful women and I realized they had probably left me alone during the week so that I could adjust, pray and contemplate.

"You can do that learning here or you can do it back in London," another nun finished what mother superior started and I needed to make sure I finished too.

"Why does there have to be war right now?" I asked and I almost stamped my foot, like a little girl, asking her mother why she has to eat all her Brussels' sprouts. "Can God make it stop? I know he didn't cause it but why can't he stop it?" I really just wanted to hear their explanation.

"Maria." This time a nun stepped forward who had been praying rosary in the corner. I had assumed she wasn't listening. It was the nun who had shown me to my room on the first day. Maria. The sour demeanor had vanished and it had been replaced by a peaceful but concerned look. "And which war should God end? Which illness should God eradicate? Heaven is where we go when we are with God. Would you have him create Heaven on Earth? If so, then you must prepare to disregard all thought processes that are not consistent with God's. Human consciousness is not of God's making because it is mingled with our own free will to choose our thoughts. Fear is not God's making because God has never been fearful and neither has God been hateful. How can God go where he doesn't exist?"

I was reminded of the temples in Egypt. Like those temples I understood that the nuns were telling me that fear is manmade and death is manmade along with every other negative feeling and action in this world.

"So you mean it is our own responsibility to create Heaven on Earth? That's how we stop the war? We effectively end the war in our own minds?"

"Yes," said Mother Superior. "God already sees Heaven on Earth, but we have to join him there. Everyday you have a choice to make. Either you choose to create Heaven around you or you choose to create your own Hell." I recognized this teaching from *A Course in Miracles* but being here now, amidst this country at war, the teaching seemed so much clearer.

"How can I choose Heaven? Hmmm." I put my thumbnail in my mouth and started chewing on it. I did that when I was deep in thought.

"Well, it's very easy." She said through a beautiful wide smile and her answer was unexpected. I thought she would direct me to read a chapter from the Bible but instead she said, "You live in love," so I took my opportunity to pounce, playing innocent I asked about sex.

"The love between a man and… woman? .... Does that count?" As expected an awkward silence descended over us, and the nuns started developing little coughs and looking for teaspoons to stir their drinks.

"How could that be possible?" A nun next to me piped up. "*That* sort of love is a filthy sin."

"Now, now," said another, worried I would become offended. "Let's calm it down a bit." They all started talking at once and I have to add that I was most bewildered at their enthusiasm for the conversation. I was honored that they felt so comfortable around me and couldn't help but chuckle at the vigor with which they spoke.

"I feel," said a chubby nun who refused to smile back at me, "that when a man and woman come together, as long as they are married of course…. Er hm…. conjugal love is an act of unity between them. It can strengthen their bond together."

"Yes!" another chimed in. "But I feel it can only work if the husband and wife also know what they want to achieve from their union and work together to reach those goals."

I was quite amazed by the insight of these women. *Where had their wisdom come from? Is this what it says in the Bible?* I thought. It sounded right to me. A relationship can only be holy if it involves the joining of minds for a common goal as opposed to the joining of two bodies. Creating children is also another holy use for sex as becoming a parent is an opportunity to clearly experience the unconditional love that God feels for us. I wished I had known this before – it would have saved me a lot of heartache. The nuns burst into a couple of different languages and were discussing away with each other. I still needed answers. I headed towards the first Maria I had met, standing by the window and in the light of the sun. I faced her eagerly, and noticed that she and I looked quite alike! She had flicked her head quickly to look at me and brown curls in a ponytail flew out from under her headdress. I saw she had hazel eyes too that glittered green in the bright sunlight. There were freckles on her nose, like mine. And when she spoke she sounded like me.

"If only my ex-boyfriends had treated me differently. If only my soul mate hadn't cheated. I wouldn't have had to go through all of this. I would be happy right now if only he hadn't left me for another woman. He made me feel like … well bad. And all these Syrian men perv on me and...” I spouted in urgency, as though the nun had the ability to wipe the past away. She interrupted me with a gentle,

“Stop, Maria.”

“It’s true though isn’t it?” I asked, defiant. Finally I had told someone how I felt but I wished those people who had done me wrong were standing in front of me then so I could tell them how they had hurt me and how what they had done was wrong. That would heal me wouldn't it?

Aware that everyone could hear us, Maria ushered me through a door into an empty hallway. Rows of paintings hung on spotless walls and the tiled floor shone. Hanging my head in embarrassment I noticed I could see my face reflected into it. My eyes were unrecognizable and not as peaceful as I thought despite being in this place that brought me comfort. They exuded a wildness about them that scared me. There’s a fine line between being lost and being onto something.

“You are on a mission for God aren’t you?” asked the nun, obviously concerned. “And you have spent many years on this journey, possibly all of your life.” I just stared back, wild eyed, not knowing what to do or say. “I will tell you now, Maria, that your entire life has been spent trying to make yourself worthy of God. You think that to find God you have to gain his love first. I know this only from listening to what you just said to me.” I nodded at Maria but inside I was ready to give up and leave the search behind me for good. *It can't be that bad – living with a void in my spirit. If I just give it a chance... millions do it every day...* "The absolute truth is that you think making someone into the bad guy will make you more worthy of God." She continued. "But you don't need someone to be the bad person for God to love you. He loves you just the way you are. You are perfect. You are loved and you are worthy of the Divine. A superhero doesn't need an enemy to prove that they are good. They are already good – goodness already lives within them."

I kept my line of sight fixed downwards. I was overwhelmed with exhaustion and relief and pain for all I had chosen to put myself through and I didn't want Maria to see. I had to maintain my composure when all I wanted to do was drop to my knees and thank her for saving my life.

"Salvation doesn't lay in making others feel guilty or blaming them. It can only happen if we take action to love others. I believe this is one of the truths of love." Maria brushed my hair away from my face and I wished I had a smooth rose quartz in my hand to focus on. Instead I held tight onto the small silver cross I wore around my neck that my nan had bought me before she passed away. I hoped it could protect me. But Maria's words left me wondering from whom? I didn't want to force anyone else to wear the mask of 'baddie' in my life. "Don't save love and forgiveness for your friends and family, Maria. Extend it and expand it outwards like a net – catch butterflies!" She tittered in joy at the image she had conjured up and with the raise of an eyebrow, signaled for me to return to my room. As I turned she called to me, "to love others is the only way to God my dear. Destroy those villain masks you distributed and stop kidding yourself that you have to win God's love. He already loves you! Very, very much!"

Chapter 45

I now thought I knew what 'to love another' meant and the beauty of it soaked me to the skin like a rain after a concert. It is the calm knowing that nobody has to be labeled bad for me to be good, whilst the meaning of life is simply to remember this. I was sitting on the balcony now outside my room filled with memories from the past couple of years of my life. Things I had read and *seen*. I saw flashbacks of the vision that had appeared to me when I called out to Magda from my bathroom floor. I remembered the peace of the people from that great circle in the desert and the way I had noticed that there was nobody more important than anyone else and I recalled the pain of the crowds when they broke away from that circle and established themselves as rich/poor, special/not special. My heart broke for us all as a bomb exploded in the distance. I was seeing the words from *A Course in Miracles* in everything happening around me. *That bomb exploded because the person who ordered its detonation is a believer in 'the separation.' He believes that the people he is killing are separate from him and he doesn't understand that he is in fact, trying to kill himself – his peace and his joy because he thinks he doesn't deserve it,* I thought, tears rolling down my face, *he feels guilt but he doesn't know why*. In a strange way, I could empathize with him. But I was conscious of the fact it couldn't possibly end there because surely this meant that just as I had viewed myself as an intruder upon Syrian society, I too must believe in the separation and had contributed somewhat to what I was seeing. *It is indeed the moment to take responsibility for what I was witness to and change my mind about it.*

I had rushed away from the nuns to write my revelations in my notebook. They yelled to come back at the same time tomorrow with understanding in their eyes. I thought they were some of the most wonderful women I had ever met and it was so strange that they had helped me to comprehend God and sex and true love.

Now I understood why I had felt so devoid of God in those moments with Saleh. I was trying to make our coupling into something it wasn't. I tried so hard to make it spiritual. I tried so hard to put all my love into it. I truly see now that I would have saved myself so much heartache if I had known that my beliefs about relationships and sex were misguided and that they wouldn't be able to complete me – not the way I had been approaching them anyway. I read so much into the act of sex and having a boyfriend and expected so much from it when really it would have served me better to enter into it with the awareness of what it cannot do for me and work from there.

The next day, I had more questions and so I approached Maria who was praying her rosary again, on the public roof terrace. It was Sunday but Saydnaya was deserted. Normally it was full of tourists from all over the world.

"Ah, darling. I thought you hadn't finished with me yet!" She laughed and gave me a light hug.

"How did you know?" I squealed, reveling in the embrace. I had been feeling so alone; sometimes it's just natural to want someone to reach out. So we leaned over the balcony, elbows on railings. Out of the corner of my eye, Maria's skin appeared to be glowing, no doubt from the clean air up in the mountains I told myself, trying not to stare. I breathed in deeply. "I wanted to ask you if you think I made the right choice in coming here. Syria I mean. I came here in the name of love and with pure trust in God." I felt my eyes tear up as I began to explain about Hassan and Saleh. Maria listened in silence and maintained her gaze over the town below. The shooting sounded very distant today.

"Do you believe in angels?" She asked quietly. I was thrown off guard by the sudden change in topic. Maybe Maria hadn't been listening to me.

"Errr of course I do. I think I saw one once." Thoughts of Magda came flying back. "I once prayed for my angel to appear to me and she appeared as a real woman who I am now really close friends with. Her name is

Magda."

"Angels are answers to prayers." Said Maria. Then she put an arm around my shoulders and added, "Did you know that every person is an angel? Every human being is an answer to someone's prayers?" I felt like my heart had dropped to my knees. This one sentence struck me as truth. Everything I had ever experienced. Every encounter I had ever had with every person came rushing back to me like rapid water. I truly thought I was hearing the voice of God. Maria continued, "Someone prayed for you to come into his or her life. Just like how you prayed for Magda. That's why you are here. Someone prayed for a native English teacher who knows about those particular exams you teach. Someone prayed for a friend. Someone prayed to see a foreigner walk the streets to comfort them. Someone prayed for a teacher to volunteer at their school. Someone prayed for a tenant for their apartment and someone prayed for a customer to buy their bread. These may sound like small things to you but at this delicate time in Syria, these are all things which one can no longer find easily." I couldn't believe the words that had left this angel's mouth. It was so simple and yet made so much sense. I had seen with my own eyes what happens when someone prays for something with all their might. "No matter what we do, small or big," Maria continued, "Someone's prayer is answered and we unknowingly teach that God is listening and smiling down on them with love." I hated crying in front of people but I couldn't help it. Maria held me close and whispered into my hair, "We are all physical manifestations of God's love for us. We are all angels."

"I have hated myself so much," I said quietly into the nun's shoulder. "I didn't understand." Maria reached into her sleeve and pulled out a tissue. She handed it to me.

"Soon the people who called you here, won't need you anymore and you will go back home." And that was the last time I saw her.

On returning to Damascus, I realized I was wrong about the nuns and convent life because it was apparent to me that those women had not disregarded their primal strength in the slightest. They had not denied the divine feminine that inhabited their spirits in a spiral dance of instinct and passion. Not only were they distinctly wise women, in tune with their feelings, but they were courageous too, to remain in the convent when religious conflicts were transpiring throughout the region. The city of Seydnaya is an easy target. It lies close to Maaloula – another Christian city with a rich, ancient history. Its people speak a variant of Aramaic – the language of Christ and the places of worship in these two cities go back to around one thousand, four hundred years ago. If a sectarian war came to Damascus, those churches would be singled out for their close connection to the Christian population. Those nuns could have left, but I knew they wouldn't. Primal woman had risen up in each of them and they had put their trust in God. They had a fire under them that roared for truth and for love.

Afterword

I feel safe and warm in the belly of the plane as it takes off into the air, leaving a light show down below in the pitch black. Some are houses and some are explosives, flashing like dying stars in a night sky. Despite knowing I had assisted many people pass their university entrance exams at international institutions and that all of the young people I worked with at the charity had gained full scholarships at several prestigious colleges across the States, I know it isn't enough. I don't want to leave Syria to her fate, but I have to embrace mine and that is to leave at this moment. My eyes are swollen with how much I have cried, ironically for that which has brought me so much happiness. Saleh, Syria, Hassan, the kids at the charity. The list could go on and on. I hold a tissue to my nose and breathe in the woody smell, lying back against the sturdy seat. I am without Saleh, but I have a new love in my life now, otherwise known as God whose love for me is so everlasting and so concrete that He would give everything He has to teach *me* – an average, broke, girl from East London, the truth about life, love and myself. I went to the desert for my dark night of the soul and I was tempted by the Devil. But I wont allow myself to feel guilt for the past. Trying to discern the reasons why I stayed in Syria during the war is like asking a cherry tree why its blossoms have to fall. When life calls out to me, I answer. And as someone who will always be inspired by the divine feminine I like to believe that when Death calls, I answer him too. As an ex-panic attack sufferer, I know what it's like to let fear of action rule me and I refuse to give into it ever again.

I now feel that life is about yielding to God's will to let him guide us so that we can become angels on Earth. Unhappiness comes when we fight him. When he tells us to love all and we only love one. When he tells us we are siblings but we see only enemies. When he says we are the same, but we notice only difference. Life is hard but life generally is more difficult without a parent's help to navigate it.

Love is a force that isn't supposed to be limited to a handful of people and we only hurt ourselves when we twist it to become a punishment rather than a true gift. Love must not become a weapon we use against ourselves where we offer it to some and withhold it from others. This is the act of enforcing masks on people that only we can see: 'cheat', 'bad', 'liar'. We want to redeem ourselves by making other people into villains so that we can be saved but this is a waste of life because God will never see the villain in them. In God's eyes we are all His children, none more important than the other and none less worthy. *What would our reality be if we could but love like God?* No doubt consistent of a million *Batmans* who don't need the *Joker* to reassure them that they are superheroes.

Glancing at the television monitor on the wall I know that in five hours I will be in calm, predictable London where people wake up at seven O'clock, get to work at nine and finish at five. They might go to the pub after, have a pint and go home to have dinner with their family. They go to bed and wake up the next day to do it all over again. And after three years of feeling as though I do not fit into Arab society, I will no doubt have moments where I believe I no longer fit into British society. I will sit in a café with a cup of tea and watch Londoners go shopping and strut about looking pretty and I will think *if only those people knew what this world has come to*. More Syrians – those I know and those I do not - will die in bombings and suffer bereavement and difficult living conditions and I will look down at my tea and wonder what part of myself created this reality. I will remember what happened with Magda and the questions I asked that only arose due to my life experiences and I will see the truth in those fleeting moments of clarity that we all have but don't know how to embrace. I am sure my friends will say,

"And your precious God? Why can't he stop the war? Why does he let it happen?" And I will tell them what the nuns taught me: God does not exist within sadness because God is happy. God does not exist within evil because God is good and God does not exist within war because God is peace. God is consistent and so is unable to represent two contradictory existences. It is us who make the choice to go places where God cannot follow.

But just as I had doubted my worth as a spiritual person a year ago: just as I had questioned my worthiness to live life wholly dedicated to the truth of *Love*, I will experience moments when I doubt that teaching. I might brush it off and say it is nonsense. I might block it out of my thoughts and wallow in despair. But it doesn't make it any less, the truth of *Love*.

For your information:

*All of the people mentioned in this story, except the wonderful nuns (that I am aware of) are now living outside of Syria.

*I debated whether to include some of the psychic experiences I had, the reason being that I don't like the idea that many people who are well known for leading spiritual movements, often talk of having 'the one psychic/spiritual experience' that leads them to being buddies with the Divine. Everyone can achieve that. It doesn't take a vision or a strange event. Psychic abilities shouldn't be synonymous with spirituality because it makes some people feel that only 'special' individuals are capable of reaching what they think are higher levels of enlightenment. In reality, we are all capable of being enlightened, just as we are all capable of being psychic. My secret to advancing my ability to tune into the energies of others is to SPEND TIME ALONE. That's it. Spend time alone and don't interact with people on superficial levels too much.

*All quotes from ***A Course in Miracles***© are from the Combined volume 2nd Edition, published in 1996, by the Foundation for Inner Peace, Viking. P.O. Box 598, Mill Valley, CA 94942-0598, www.acim.org and info@acim.org.

Thank you to:
Maria.L, Julakha.S, Joe.G, T.S, Beth.C, Farhan.M, Yamen.A, Karim.Y, Raluca.D, Chris.W, Tayo.O, Charlene.M, Eileen.A, Sajjad.F, Magda.S and David for the inspiration & friendship.

Thank you to my lovely family, here and passed.
Thank you for taking care of me.

Thank you Mother-Father God, Goddess, Angel Magda. I know I haven't been the 'most intelligent' student you've ever had! Thanks for your patience!

I love you Syria! Thank you for having me! Many of us are working to help you end the war by changing our minds. May *Love* stay with you.

Due to maintaining their privacy and their families' safety, I am not able to use the real names of the people who have passed away.

RIP

Dearest K & B.

I know we will be reunited in the Damascus in the stars one day.

I will end this with a dedication to Tyson.J.

You still have my heart.

Thank you for being a superhero in the story of my life.

36239767R00187

Made in the USA
Middletown, DE
28 October 2016